TOTAL
ENVIRONMENTAL CONTROL

THE ECONOMICS OF CROSS-MEDIA
POLLUTION TRANSFERS

Related Pergamon Titles of Interest

Full details of all Pergamon publications/free specimen copy of any Pergamon journal available on request from your nearest Pergamon office.

TOTAL ENVIRONMENTAL CONTROL

THE ECONOMICS OF CROSS-MEDIA POLLUTION TRANSFERS

BY

JULIAN LOWE
Senior Lecturer, School of Management, University of Bath

DAVID LEWIS
*formerly Research Officer, School of Management,
University of Bath*

and

MARTIN ATKINS
Principal Lecturer, Department of Business Studies, Trent Polytechnic

PERGAMON PRESS

OXFORD · NEW YORK · TORONTO · SYDNEY · PARIS · FRANKFURT

U.K.	Pergamon Press Ltd., Headington Hill Hall, Oxford OX3 0BW, England
U.S.A.	Pergamon Press Inc., Maxwell House, Fairview Park, Elmsford, New York 10523, U.S.A.
CANADA	Pergamon Press Canada Ltd., Suite 104, 150 Consumers Road, Willowdale, Ontario M2J 1P9, Canada
AUSTRALIA	Pergamon Press (Aust.) Pty. Ltd., P.O. Box 544, Potts Point, N.S.W. 2011, Australia
FRANCE	Pergamon Press SARL, 24 rue des Ecoles, 75240 Paris, Cedex 05, France
FEDERAL REPUBLIC OF GERMANY	Pergamon Press GmbH, 6242 Kronberg-Taunus, Hammerweg 6, Federal Republic of Germany

First edition 1982

Library of Congress Cataloging in Publication Data

Lowe, Julian.
Total environmental control.
1. Environmental policy—Economic aspects. 2. Environ
-mental protection—Economic aspects. 3. Factory and
trade waste—Economic aspects. I. Lewis, David.
II. Atkins, Martin. III. Title.
HC79.E5L68   1982   363.7'3   82-9827
ISBN 0-08-026276-7

In order to make this volume available as economically and as rapidly as possible the authors' typescripts have been reproduced in their original forms. This method unfortunately has its typographical limitations but it is hoped that they in no way distract the reader.

Printed in Great Britain by A. Wheaton & Co. Ltd., Exeter

This book is dedicated to all those politicians, public servants, businessmen and academics who see a clean environment as a means rather than an end.

PART I

Introduction and Evidence

CHAPTER 1

The Cross-media Problem

INTRODUCTION

In order to achieve ambient environmental quality standards, emission standards are set by governments for pollutants from various sources. Whilst these limitations on discharges may correct the immediate environmental problems at which they were initially directed, the limitations themselves often have secondary impacts beyond the intended improvements in air or water quality. Certain control technologies, aimed at achieving specific limits to pollution, generate new waste streams which may themselves have adverse environmental effects. Such new waste streams are what we refer to as cross-media pollution transfers. It is likely that they are a feature of all environmental control situations. Consequently the real question is to evaluate how important this kind of transfer is in the context of the overall environmental problem.

It should first be emphasised that cross-media transfers must be the rule rather than the exception. This is because, in keeping with the 'Law of Conservation of Mass', residuals from a production process cannot be destroyed. Their destination can be altered but ultimately they must reenter the flow of materials within the environment. In general we would expect the mass of residuals to increase with increases in production, although the manufacturing technology may be such as to delay the entry of residuals into the environment by some form of storage. These are in essence the arguments of Ayres and Kneese (I) who were prominent in emphasising the generality of external costs and thus the generality of environmental damage stemming from production. The external effect of a residuals flow may be positive, zero or negative depending on whether the resultant material is itself valuable, a nuisance or neither. Similarly, the use of a control device to change the nature of the waste stream may have a net impact which is positive, zero or negative. This needs some further clarification of what is meant by economic damage. Not only does the Law of Conservation of Mass imply that residuals cannot be destroyed, but also by virtue of entropy we might expect that the total mass of residuals would increase following control, even though the resultant damage would normally be reduced.

3

It should be emphasised here that we should concern ourselves only with the economic damage caused by pollution and not by the pollution itself. In order for the concept of damage to be meaningful in a decision-making context, we must consider only the effects of pollution upon people, and avoid the obvious - but common - fallacy of treating the preservation of a clean environment as an end in itself. This point cannot be over-emphasised - a clean environment is not an end, but only a means, and any measure designed to improve it must be viewed as such. The most damaging pollutant is the one whose avoidance is most highly valued by individuals, and in comparing alternative combinations of pollution streams the least damaging one is the stream whose overall avoidance is least valued by all those affected.

This is, however, clearly a source of conflict since because economic damage tends to be viewed in the aggregate (see Chapter 6 on cost-benefit analysis) there will frequently be individuals or groups who feel that whilst pollution control has diverted a waste stream in the best manner for society as a whole, the damage inflicted on one group may be much more than before. The issue of cross-media transfers is not one of preventing transfers taking place, but of transforming pollutants in the least damaging manner. Imperfection in environmental goods markets is at the heart of the environmental problem, and the issue of cross-media transfers centres around an exacerbation of these imperfections, so that identification of source of the damage becomes even more difficult. Since pollution streams are often redirected by public agencies, recourse to damage is similarly more complicated.

This problem has, of course, been recognised as being of considerable potential importance. In the U.S. and Europe, various moves have been made to develop integrated and comprehensive approaches to environmental management, although the instruments and policing of any resultant policy have not so far been sufficiently sophisticated. Indeed some scepticism about the practical impact of any change in policy direction has been expressed by various authors. (2) Nevertheless the formation of the E.P.A. in the U.S. was seen as a move towards a more comprehensive and integrated approach to environmental management, whilst in the U.K. the fifth Royal Commission on Environmental Pollution suggested that the pervasiveness of cross-media transfers was an important reason for considering an integrated pollution inspectorate. (3)

CROSS-MEDIA PROBLEMS : SOME DEFINITIONS

Most analyses of the cross-media problem start with some relatively straight forward view of what constitutes cross-media pollution transfers. However, it is probably necessary to define terms a little more widely, since one cannot distinguish in principle between transfer within a medium and transfers between media. For example, transfers within media over time, are conceptually closely allied to the transfers that occur between media at one point in time. What is really crucial is that the damage caused by pollution may be diverted by location, time, environmental medium or receiving group, in such a way that the secondary effects are not always properly considered in public policy evaluation. This may be because of loosely defined legal property rights, an absence of strict liability being applied through the courts, or different and competitive agencies policing the various media separately. The secondary effects may also be missed merely because of inadequate surveillance and enforcement. The common factor, however, is that the pollution stream has in some way been diverted.

It is this common factor which will be the sole basis of the definition
of a cross-media transfer and which is adopted here. The framework of
analysis is based upon a comparison of different waste streams, and in
principle it matters not for the purpose whether one is comparing one form
of air pollution with another, or a form of air pollution with a form of
water pollution. The comparison should in each case be based upon the same
criteria of economic damage, and only the practical difficulty of assessing
this damage may differ. If transfers of pollution from one medium to
another have received more attention in the literature than transfers within
a medium, or transfers in the time of pollution, then this may only be
because the former is the problem which has the potential to bring different
regulatory agencies into conflict. All types of transfer involving a
diverted waste stream are included in the definition of cross-media
transfer to be used here, and both inter- and intra-medium transfers are
examined.

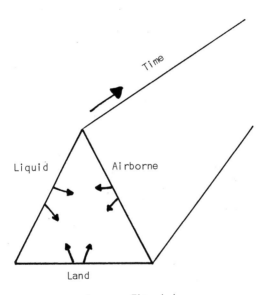

Fig. 1.1

An assessment of cross-media transfers can be made with the use of the
framework above. Only three basic media are used for illustrative purposes
although of course there are subsets of these three covering aesthetic
problems, noise, odour, etc. Transfers of pollutants may be made between
any of the media and time dimensions. The process is continuing and
dynamic since pollutants cannot be destroyed so that there are feedbacks
from the secondary media to the primary media. For example a liquid waste
may be sludged and dumped on a landfill site, later rainfall or groundwater
movement may leach out the site and return the pollutant to the waterborne
environment after a time lag. Any control equipment used in the transformation or transportation of the pollutant may also generate pollutants, so

the problem is not only continuing but may possibly result in a divergent or convergent geometric progression. Clearly under these conditions evaluation is crucial but also potentially difficult.

Two important terms that should be defined and distinguished are transfers and trade-offs. Transfers of potential pollutants may occur for any number of reasons. Pollutants may be washed out of the atmosphere by precipitation, odours may occur when sewage is collected and treated, and liquid pollutants may arise in manufacturing because of the treatment of an airborne residual for economic and production reasons. Thus a transfer merely relates to a physical change in the media destination of the pollutant. Consequently transfers are general and occur in the process of production, pollution control and independently due to changes in meteorological conditions etc. It might, of course, be claimed that they only occur because of a policy of no control. This may be so, but it is still worthwhile making the contrast between transfers and trade-offs which are the result of an explicit act of choice by public or private decision-makers. This will usually involve choosing between alternative technologies of control. Transfers are thus physical phenomena which can be measured in various ways; trade-offs, on the other hand, are distinct economic phenomena and should be measured in units of environmental damage. The distinction is important, since public policy always involves some degree of choice.

Trade-offs may arise because of an end of line control being adopted or because one process rather than another is adopted in the first place. An example of a trade-off arising from the use of end of line technology would be when a wet scrubbing device is used to clean airborne wastes and generates liquid effluent. Trade-offs might occur at the very beginning when certain processes are favoured above others by planners. Thus the siting of a factory and consents on the type of equipment to be used could ultimately be responsible for trade-offs resulting from what could be deemed 'in-plant' changes.

It is important to notice that an inter-media trade-off may also be accompanied by another form of trade-off, in cases where several forms of cross-media transfers can be present simultaneously. In particular there may be inter-temporal trade-offs when a pollutant is transformed such that its impact on the environment may be reduced but may also be delayed. Some forms of tipping would surely fall into this category. Cross-media trade-offs may also have a social distributional impact − either because the control technology shifts the pollutant from one media to another or from one geographic location to another. Finally there may be locational trade-offs per se, due to the explicit choice of the environmental control system between policies of concentration or of dispersion of pollutants.
Currently in the U.K. it seems that some airborne residuals are subject to heavy concentration in particular locations. Thus trade-offs are made when public choice changes the nature of the pollutant, its form, the receiving media and its location.

Not only do we have to consider the transfer of pollutants over time, location and recipient income group via the media air, water and land, but also within these media we can distinguish problems of odour, aesthetics and noise for instance. These can be frequently under estimated but, maybe the really important cross-media impacts of pollution at Battersea Power Station for instance, were not those caused by a scrubbing of sulphur oxides in the stack gases which resulted in the River Thames being polluted (all because the King was worried about the umpleasant air drifting over to Buckingham Palace), but rather the aesthetically displeasing and dominating cooling towers which were used to ameliorate the heat pollution in the River Thames. In the end these must have obscured some valued views, albeit not regal ones.

Cross-media effects are then general environmental phenomena, and the rest of this book is concerned with evaluating these from both a theoretical, administrative and empirical point of view.

VOLUNTARY SOLUTIONS TO CROSS-MEDIA PROBLEMS

If, of course, cross-media transfers of pollution did not constitute damage to environmental media where property rights are confused and indistinct, then the 'problem' of cross-media effects could be solved by the usual processes of litigation and damages awarded through the courts, since it would not matter which media were ultimately damaged as long as the polluter could be identified. Cross-media transfers would continue but the claim that they were distorting the allocation of resources could only be made if there were other imperfections in the market between polluters and the pollution receivers. Thus, for instance, the firm scrubbing gases and then discharging to the sewer pays for the damage caused because of the distinct nature of property rights inherent in the contract between the discharger and receiver. However, most environmental resources are the subject of, at least a degree, of common ownership and so cross-media effects become a public policy problem. To compound their complexity it should also be noted that many cross-media transfers may be difficult to trace to source. Consequently whilst their impact can be demonstrated in theory, the generally inadequate policing of environmental regulations may be reinforced by the confusion caused by the damage being transferred between or within various environmental media.

The alternative way of achieving an optimal allocation of resources between the environment and goods markets is, of course, via a private bargaining solution. This approach has come in for heavy criticism because of its lack of realism, collective goods problems, and the implications for income distribution.

The voluntary approach to the externality problem revolves around two basic principles. Firstly, it is suggested that since in cases of environmental pollution there are gainers and losers, it should be possible for the two parties to bargain in such a way that the losers can bribe the gainers to reduce pollution levels. Consequently an allocation of economic resources, the same as should be sought by state intervention, could be achieved as the losers from pollution could bribe the gainers up to the point where marginal private benefit of production is equal to its marginal social cost. Secondly, it is suggested that the outcome of such a bargaining process is invariant with respect to the legal ownership rights of the environmental resources that are used both for life support and as a waste sink.

Whilst these arguments have considerable intuitive appeal it is doubtful whether they are either internally consistent or could serve as the basis of policy towards the environment. A major facet of the approach is that it largely assumes away the transaction costs and organisational problems of getting those impacted by the pollution to act as a group. Even if it were assumed that they could act in unison then the negotiated agreement becomes a bilateral monopoly case which a priori is likely to lead to an indeterminate solution. Finally the possibility of threats could also disturb any cosy notions of equilibrium. It is almost axiomatic that good bargainers do not disclose their bargaining limits - consequently threats become a likely aspect of negotiation. In the presence of threats any agreement is only likely to be optimal by chance. Indeed threats may induce polluting behaviour beyond that level profitable for the polluter in order that his threats become more believable in the next negotiating round.

The independence of ownership rights and the level of activity also seems a dubious proposition both in theory and practice. In the long run the bribe revenues collected by the polluter (if the ownership rights had been ascribed to him) would act as an inducement for new firms to enter the industry and thus change production levels and the allocation of resources. Finally, a compelling reason to reject the negotiated solution is that, in view of the long run existence of serious externality problems that demand some form of government intervention, the voluntary approach has clearly not been workable.

However, one area where it might be expected that there is some scope for a private solution, is in the case of cross-frontier pollution transfers (which is really just a special case of cross-media transfers) since in this area the source and recipient of the pollution need not cause too many problems and, more importantly, the collective goods barrier for the bribing party should, in the case of a nation acting alone, cease to be an issue. Thus since Canada feels its wheatfields and forestry are adversely affected by the smoke stacks of U.S. industry, and if the latter wont increase emission control, then it would seem economically efficient for the Canadians to subsidize some U.S. pollution control. This has not yet occurred, but in a similar case in Europe the problems caused to the Dutch by French Alkali pits discharging to the Rhine has been the subject of financial negotiations involving compensation for the French if they reduce the scale of their activity.

One of the major problems of incorporating cross-media effects into regulatory processes is that there is sometimes considerable uncertainty in identifying the source of pollution. This is particularly so in the case of dumping where the environmental impact may not be seen for many years. If control agencies set standards or charges on the basis of economic damage caused, then they have to forecast what this will be. This may prove to be the major stumbling block for comprehensive approaches to environmental management, and this issue is discussed in the last two chapters of this book.

Ultimately since pollution has to end up somewhere, controls should aim at achieving a mix between the least damaging and least cost methods of disposal. We argue throughout this book that some estimate of the damage has therefore to be made for a proper understanding of the effects on resource allocation of cross-media pollution transfer. However, we note at this point that a considerable amount of research in the U.S. has looked at the problem in another way. This work by Spofford, Russell and Kelley (4) and later Kneese and Bower (5) on residuals management in the lower Delaware valley points up the issue of cost minimising rather than cost and benefit optimising. They investigated the costs of control at plant level for achieving given ambient quality standards in different media. This approach leads to estimates of the extra cost of achieving (say) a given level of air quality for various assumptions about water quality standards that have to be maintained. Not surprisingly a sharply increasing marginal cost schedule is revealed under these conditions. This is dealt with later on in the concluding chapter of this book.

However, an important question arises about where should the analysis stop. Clearly any assumptions about increasing standards in one medium are bound to have important repercussions on the costs of control in another medium unless the residuals can be completely recycled or eliminated. Even then the secondary environmental costs concerned with the production of the pollution control plant itself, the energy and materials used in its manufacture, should all enter the equation. This sort of approach is important as it points to the size of secondary effects of various control systems. However, possibly the more relevant question for decision-making purposes is the one that merely ascertains the extent to which the cross-media trade-offs are positive, negative or neutral. As long as they are negative then maintaining the existing administrative system may well be expedient.

CONCLUSIONS

The problem of cross-media transfers is an important one to consider, because not all environmental media are adequately or similarly controlled and protected. Consequently under any piecemeal system there is always a danger that pressure from one environmental agency will impact adversely on another part of the environment that is either not properly protected or may not even have been adequately defined so as to warrant protection. Currently, for instance, control seems toughest in those areas where possible irreversible effects exist or at least where they are given most publicity! This might mean that control bodies pursue policies for certain pollutants in certain media that are designed to eliminate them at almost all costs - even though the economic damage at the margin might not warrant this. Whereas secondary damage caused to - for example - the landscape or aesthetics might be largely ignored even where there is a substantial degree of economic damage, on the other hand inequitable controls between media may result from ignorance about pollution in effluent streams and its effect on the environment. Whatever the reasons and whether these are political, economic or technical it is likely that control of pollution does sometimes cause perverse cross-media effects. Thus the rest of this book deals with the evidence firstly at an aggregate and later at a case study level. Consideration is then given to alternatives which may be useful in providing decision-makers with information on which to base their decisions. Finally we consider how, if at all, cross-media transfers should affect the operation of public policy in the area of environmental management.

REFERENCES

1. Ayres, R.U. and Kneese, A.V. (1969). Production, Consumption and Externalities. American Economic Review. p.282
2. Lowe, J. and Lewis, D. (1980). Comprehensive versus Piecemeal Approaches to Environmental Control. International Journal of Social Economics. Vol.7 No.5.
3. The Royal Commission on Environmental Pollution. Fifth Report, 1976
4. Spofford, W.O., Russel, C.S. and Kelley, R. (1976). Environmental Quality Management: An Application to the Lower Delaware Valley. Washington, D.C. Resources for the Future Inc.
5. Kneese, A.V. and Bower, B.T. (1979). Environmental Quality and Residuals Management. Resources for the Future. John Hopkins, University Press.

CHAPTER 2

Transfers to Water — a Case Study

INTRODUCTION

It seems likely that almost all instances of cross-media transfers of pollution concern the waterborne environment in some way, whether involving a transfer to or from the water medium. For this reason it was considered important to gather and analyse information pertaining to cross-media transfers from the authorities responsible for the regulation of water resources. To this end, meetings were held with representatives from each of the ten Regional Water Authorities in England and Wales, and in each case the representatives included a senior member of the authority's scientific or technical department. The objective was to assess the way in which cross-media transfers of pollution involving water were perceived, in terms of nature, extent and importance, by the regulatory agencies.

'WET SCRUBBING'

The use of 'wet scrubbing' (or gas cleaning) devices in various industries in order to reduce airborne emissions of pollutants would appear to be a clear-cut case of an air-water transfer of pollution, so we were anxious to gauge the extent to which these methods of control are used throughout England and Wales. It was somewhat surprising to learn that, so far as the Water Authorities were aware, wet scrubbing is not a major source of industrial effluent except, perhaps, in the Midlands and South Wales. In fact the Water Authorities would not always be aware of the exact volume and chemical nature of discharges arising from wet scrubbing whether going to a river or to a sewer, since consents are typically issued for the combined emission from a whole plant, only a small proportion of which may emanate from a scrubbing operation. Nevertheless many of the authorities looked into this matter on our behalf, and only two authorities considered there to be more than six such discharges to a river within their jurisdiction, whilst one region did not know of any instances at all. In aggregate it seems unlikely that there are more than fifty wet scrubbers discharging to river and these discharges amount to considerably less than half of one per cent of all discharges excluding cooling water. The authority that had the largest number of wet scrubbers reported that this discharge was two megalitres per day and that the total discharge of trade effluent to river was 500 megalitres per day. Data from all water authorities able to make an estimate of the relative impact of scrubbing effluent are given in Table 2.1 below. It was emphasised however, that whilst wet scrubbers were not in general a major problem encountered, the authorities were aware of the potential dangers from transferring pollution in this way.

TABLE 2.1   Discharges of 'Wet Scrubbing' Effluent to Rivers and Coastal Waters

Authority	Total No. of discharges to rivers (excluding cooling water)	Estimate of No. of 'Wet Scrubbers' discharging to river	Estimate of No of 'Wet Scrubbers' discharging directly to coastal waters
1	221	5	1
2	904	18	1
3	N/A*	1	2
4	68	0	0
5	722	1	0
6	189	10	0
7	N/A*	1	0

*   Described as 'few' in Water Quality Report

Iron and Steel and Fertilizers appear to be the largest users of wet scrubbers, whilst other activities involved include petrochemicals, metal smelting, domestic and industrial refuse incineration, and iron founding. Naturally the effect of any particular discharge will depend upon its constituents, as well as whether it is emitted to a river or a sewer and what degree of treatment, if any, it receives.

TIPPING

The second major sphere of interest to us was the potential solid-water transfer associated with the tipping of industrial and domestic wastes. These wastes can vary from the most inert and harmless substance to the moxt toxic. Under the Control of Pollution Act all sites used for tipping must have licences, and the possibility of surface waters being affected will be an important factor in determining licence conditions. Many tips are owned and operated by Local Authorities, and whilst these normally cater for domestic refuse, some also take industrial waste of certain kinds. In a few cases local councils do have tips specifically for industrial usage, but more commonly this waste is deposited on a tip owned by the firm itself or by contractors, who often arrange for transportation as well as dumping. Where contractors are used, the firm employing them may well not be aware of the final destination of their residual materials, so that the waste and the tip become effectively (though not necessarily legally)

the contractors' sole responsibility. The Control of Pollution Act, when
fully implemented, will require tip operators to keep detailed records of
substances deposited, in order to ensure compliance with licence provisions.

There are basically two ways in which surface waters may be adversely
affected by tips, through surface run-offs and through leaching. The former
is a common - indeed almost inevitable - problem associated mainly with
domestic refuse tips, insofar as rainfall will always lead to some surface
materials from tips being absorbed and to this flowing into nearby streams
or rivers. With more toxic substances, tipping should always be undertaken
in such a way as to minimise such occurrences, but this is not normally
economically viable for less dangerous materials such as ordinary domestic
waste. However Water Authorities do not underestimate the potential damage
from run-offs even of domestic wastes, and this will be a factor in
determining tip locations. The magnitude of any such problem can only be
determined by sampling of streams, which is in itself fairly easily done,
but the difficulty arises from the fact that it is not always possible to
distinguish the source of any particular pollutant present.

Much more complex is the problem of tip leachate. The propensity of a tip
to leach depends essentially upon the geological features of its location
and the steps, if any, taken to reduce the likelihood of such a problem
arising. Our information from the Water Authorities was that most tips
would be monitored periodically by means of sampling surface waters, but
that boreholes would only be made where there was a persistent problem, or
where a tip received highly toxic wastes. Drilling boreholes is a costly
operation, but it is the only way of regularly monitoring underground
aquifers. There have in the past been instances of the leaching of highly
toxic materials into surface waters, but improvements in the standard of
supervision of poisonous waste tips should reduce the likelihood of such
occurrences in the future. Nevertheless, even leaching from domestic
refuse tips can have discernible effects on watercourses.

There is a very important time dimension to the problem of leachate, since
it may take many years - even decades - for tip liquors to find their way
through the various strata of the earth's crust into surface waters. It
is for this reason that boreholes are necessary in cases where it is
suspected that leaching may be taking place. Of course the appearance of
toxic material in a watercourse will have particularly serious potential
consequences if drinking water is abstracted downstream.

Fish kills, or the disappearance of fish caused by the presence of leachate
with a high B.O.D. are both events treated by Water Authorities as being
serious in nature. In fact, the impact of the absence of fish from a short
stretch of water may be quite minimal, affecting only a few fishermen, and
remedial expenditure sometimes seems hard to justify in economic terms.
It was remarked to us concerning one piece of water on which expensive
remedial action had been taken, that it would have been cheaper to send
all the fishermen who used the water on an all expenses paid trip to Ireland
every year, than to preserve the fish population. Nevertheless, whether for
reasons of lobbying or feeling of statutory obligation, large sums are often
spent on the protection of fisheries. The fact that this fishing is the
subject of private property rights may not be unimportant in these decisions.

Most Authorities we spoke to were experiencing a few cases of leachate
reaching surface waters, and whilst an attempt to remedy the situation would
almost always be made, it would often not be completely effective. This
might be because of expense, or simply because of the time needed for

leachate which has passed the 'control point' to find its way into the stream. A typical approach to solving leachate problems is to construct a trench on the perimeter of the tip, which will act as a lagoon for the tip liquor. This can be tankered away for treatment or alternatively be dealt with by some form of on-site aeration. The construction of perimeter trenches is a drastic solution, but is often the only one possible where leaching is by means of underground percolation. Less expensively, it may sometimes be feasible to intercept the liquor at a point or points near to where it enters the stream, and divert it to sewer.

Leaching can be a problem on both domestic and industrial refuse disposal sites. Almost all industrial activities generate some form of solid residual, but some industries tend to produce wastes with especially dangerous constituents. The Metal Finishing Industry in particular generates sludges with highly toxic characteristics, and we were told by the Severn-Trent Water Authority that in the West Midlands much of the waste tipped comes from this source. Our initial emphasis on concern with solid-water transfers from metal finishing appears from our discussion to have been justified. Any leaching from tips on which sludges containing cyanide or arsenic compounds or with high concentrations of heavy metals have been dumped, would be potentially a very serious threat to the waterborne environment. In fact metal finishing wastes are normally tipped on the same sites as many other industrial residuals, so it is not always possible to isolate the effects of such wastes.

Whereas the use of wet scrubbing did not prove to be a major source of water pollution, our discussions have shown that run-offs and more especially leaching from tips are important problems, and occupy a substantial number of man-hours in Water Authorities' work programmes. There was a considerable degree of consensus amongst those representatives that we spoke to, that tips are the most important sources of cross-media transfers involving water. Most of the problems encountered involved the deoxygenation of a watercourse or a growth of sewage fungus, resulting from a leachate with a high B.O.D. value. The other form of pollution which arose in a few cases was a high Ammoniacal Nitrogen, but in no case was potable water extraction threatened by tip leachate. Evidence that we collected from the Water Authorities suggests that any solution to a leachate problem must consist firstly of collecting the liquor, and secondly of disposing of it. Leachate may be collected by the construction of a trench which acts as a lagoon or in a sump and subsequently pumped to a lagoon. Once collected, in some cases the liquor was taken away by tanker to a sewage treatment plant or to a sea outfall. In other cases there was some form of on-site treatment, which either simply took the form of aeration, or involved pumping the liquor back to the top of the tip in order to encourage exidation.

SEWAGE TREATMENT AND DISPOSAL

Sewage treatment and disposal is one of the three areas of responsibility of the Regional Water Authorities. There are innumerable ways in which this function might be discharged, ranging from full treatment at one extreme to simply running sewers directly into the sea without any form of treatment at the other. The important, if somewhat obvious, point to be made is that sewage treatment does not necessarily eliminate the damage potential of the effluent being subjected to it. In fact treatment normally involves the conversion of a stream of liquid waste into a sludge or solid.

There is, therefore, a basic trade-off associated with sewage treatment, involving the alternatives of a more damaging final liquid effluent on the one hand, and a more toxic sludge residual on the other hand, depending upon the degree of treatment the waste receives. This choice can be viewed as one between 'concentrate and contain' (the more toxic sludge) and 'dilute and disperse' (less intensive effluent treatment). The former policy, involving more treatment, appears to be the preferred one in the U.K. for more toxic effluents since the dispersal of untreated or only partly treated liquid effluent is fraught with dangers.

There are four main ways of disposing of sewage sludge:- spreading on land as an agricultural fertiliser, incineration, depositing on sacrificial land, or dumping at sea. All of these involve some further transfer of pollution. Most Water Authorities dispose of a substantial proportion of their sludge on agricultural land, since this is easily the cheapest option, though Authorities such as Thames and Severn-Trent with large conurbations are unable to use this method for the majority of their sludge for obvious reasons. For example, most of London's sludge is taken down the Thames in barges and dumped in the North Sea.

The spreading of sewage sludge, whilst in principle and normally in practice offering a solution which transforms a pollutant into a useful good, is fraught with dangers in two respects which can be considered as separate issues. In the first instance, there can be relatively high concentrations of heavy metals present and for this reason guidelines concerning the maximum concentration of these metals which are permissible in sludge to be spread agriculturally are laid down, and are observed by all the Water Authorities in England and Wales. This policy necessitates that strict maximum concentrations are imposed on discharges of effluent entering a sewage works whose sludge will be disposed of in this way, which in turn may force firms to instal their own pre-treatment plant. This plant will generate its own sludge with a high metal content and commercial organisations may be less meticulous in the way they dispose of their sludge than are Water Authorities, whose business it is to know the dangers associated with high metal concentrations. This point is made in order to illustrate the fact that guidelines which are in themselves wholy reasonable and sensible, may be counter-productive if the whole problem is not viewed in a broad context.

It was suggested to us by one representative that effluent treatment in all its stages should be undertaken by the Water Authority, at a charge reflecting cost, because they were the organisation best qualified to do this job efficiently. It may be desirable that the agency responsible for protecting the waterborne environment is the body that makes the decision as to how particular effluents are dealt with, rather than a commercial organisation with other objectives. There may also in some cases be economies of scale to be derived from different effluents being treated collectively, though the converse may also sometimes be true. In any case, the argument that treatment should where possible be undertaken by the Water Authority obviously carries some weight.

The second issue concerning the spreading of sludge on land is associated with the time allowed for settlement and digestion before disposal. The majority of representatives were of the opinion that 3-6 months was the minimum settlement period which reduced the bacterial content of the sludge sufficiently for it to be safely spread. However at least one authority allows the disposal of raw sludge on agricultural land, and is of the view that there is little danger of run-offs adversely affecting watercourses provided that the quantity spread and the place of deposit are adequately controlled. In fact those that we spoke to emphasised that run-offs from the excessive application of fertilisers in the fields are a much more serious problem. Perhaps more important than any threat to watercourses from the spreading of undigested sludge is the possibility of 'take-up' by plants of bacteria such a salmonella, which could be transferred to food. The extent to which this is possible or likely is currently the subject of considerable debate, and we pass no judgement on this matter. What can be asserted is that there is a cost saving to be made by reducing the sludge settlement period, and that there are possible dangers of spreading undigested sludge on agricultural land.

The dumping of sludge at sea is an alternative form of disposal which is quite widely practiced in the more urban areas of the U.K., and can be little more expensive than agricultural spreading. Of course there is a danger of pollution of the sea or of coastlines arising from the dumping, but the Ministry of Agriculture, Fisheries and Food in a report on the Thames Water Authority's use of the North Sea for this purpose, was of the opinion that little damage was perceptible.

The incineration of sludge is a much more costly process, and inherently involves a further cross-media transfer of pollution from solid to air. Air pollution from an incinerator will normally be controlled in some way, sometimes by a wet arrestment device, resulting in a further air-water transfer. One interesting case in the Midlands was brought to our attention, where a sludge incineration plant employs a wet scrubber whose effluent is discharged to sewer. The whole cycle then commences again, since some of the effluent is transformed into a sludge which is incinerated. There is a partially closed loop including water-solid-air-water transformation of pollution, perhaps the 'ultimate' case of cross-media transfers. This is an extreme example, but it does illustrate the point that sewage treatment is by nature a transfer, and not a 'destruction' process.

The fourth major alternative for sludge disposal, the use of sacrificial dumping land has potential problems which have been discussed earlier in the section on tips in general. We are faced, then, with a range of alternative forms of cross-media transfer to which the sludge can be subjected. The problem is to compare the environmental impact and economic cost of each.

Sludge disposal would certainly appear to constitute the major area of cross-media transfer associated with sewage treatment, but there is also the question of odours from treatment works, which are often the subject of complaints. These constitute water-air (aesthetic) transfers, and steps are sometimes taken to alleviate the nuisance by means of masking sprays which have a supposedly 'pleasant' smell. These devices do not chemically react with gaseous emissions, but rather are designed to 'drown' them. It seems that the odour problem arises mainly from the primary treatment stage, so that no substantial trade-off exists between more treatment and more smell, or between less water pollution and less airborne (aesthetic) pollution. It has also been suggested that the unsightly appearance of treatment plants and the noise associated with their operation constitute further cross-media transfers.

Some Water Authority representatives spoke to us of instances where permission had been given for residential development in close proximity to existing sewage treatment plants. It seems to the authors that the harmful effects of such plants arising from cross-media transfers of pollution could often be reduced by a better use of planning controls.

Up to this point, sewage treatment and its various associated transfers of pollution have been considered. An alternative to treatment, as such, is to discharge the sewers directly into the sea. There are numerous sites in England where trunk sewers run into the sea just beyond the low water mark, and some in South Wales where they do not even extend that far. The effect of this course of action in terms of environmental impact is difficult to assess, but there certainly appears to be some influence on the sea and rather more on the coastline, particularly where there are holiday beaches. Even this alternative of 'no treatment', then, involves a transfer of pollution of some kind. The choice is really one between odours and sludge disposal problems on the one hand, and the damage caused by disposal to sea on the other.

Authorities are empowered - indeed obliged - to make charges reflecting the true cost of treating industrial discharges to sewer. The nature of charges made can influence the incidence of cross-media transfers of pollution in essentially two ways. In the first place it is quite clear that the higher the charges made for liquid effluent, the less likely are firms to transfer pollution to this medium. Less obvious, however, is the opportunity for dischargers to reduce their total liquid effluent bill by diluting or concentrating the discharges. Of course, to the extent that such a policy reduces the real cost of treatment by the Water Authority, it is quite economically justified. Unfortunately no charging policy can perfectly reflect the cost of treatment through its various stages, but a brief discussion of the basis of charges is included below as an indication of their effectiveness in reflecting costs. Any imperfection gives rise to the opportunity of a deadweight economic loss being imposed on society by a firm reducing its charges without reducing the cost of treating its effluent. Practice does vary from one authority to another, but most base their charging system upon some variation of the 'Mogden Formula'.

OTHER ISSUES

Whilst wet scrubbers can be used in the power generation industry a much more common form of cross-media transfer involves the employment of cooling towers. The potential for damage to rivers through the emission of hot water may be considerable, and Water Authorities normally require steps to be taken to ensure that river temperature is not raised by more than about 9°C. The problem of thermal pollution is particularly acute on the Trent and Thames, so that many power stations are required to instal cooling towers in order to reduce the temperature of the waste water which they discharge. Cooling towers in almost any location may be a blight on the landscape, so that the insistence on temperature standards for emissions causes a water-solid (aesthetic) transfer of pollution. This appears to be an interesting case of a trade-off between thermal water pollution, perhaps resulting in fish kills as well as steam rising from the river, and visual disamenity of cooling towers.

Anaerobicity and autrophication are themselves a possible source of a water-air transfer of pollution, as they cause accompanying odour problems. One or two of our major rivers do become anaerobic for short stretches during hot weather, though the problem is not extensive and it is possible to alleviate it by means of injecting Oxygen. Eutrophication is a little more widespread, particularly in parts of the country where rivers are slow flowing, and generally Water Authorities felt that cross-media transfers of this kind from water to air were unusual but could nevertheless occur.

It became clear to us at an early stage of our enquiries that tipping was the single most important source of cross-media transfers of pollution to water. It does seem, therefore, that a brief consideration of the alternatives to the use of landfill sites would be worthwhile. So far as domestic refuse is concerned, the only other really viable option appears to be incineration, and many Local Authorities do operate incinerators for part of their waste disposal activities. It would not be untrue to assert that the relatively high cost of incineration would be sufficient to deter Authorities from using this method of disposal if adequate suitable landfill space were available, ignoring any environmental considerations. However, just as tipping has a potential impact on the water medium, so incinceration will cause airborne emissions which may be partially transferred to water if a wet arrestment device were employed. Precise quantitative comparisons of the two strategies in terms of impact are not possible, but a point to be borne in mind is that, after incineration, about 20% by volume and nearly 50% by mass of the original waste remain to be disposed of by tipping.[1]

CONCLUSIONS

The incidence of transfers of pollution from other media to water is substantial. In terms of avoidable harmful effects, tips are the source of the greatest concern, whilst the other topics considered above are all the potential causes of environmental damage. There is no question of any Water Authority transferring pollution to a medium outside its responsibility as a matter of policy, though some transfer of damage is sometimes unavoidable where there are financial constraints, and an example of this is the discharge of untreated sewage to the sea, rather than the construction of costly treatment plants. The most important cross-media transfers all involve water, and Water Authorities appear to us to have both the desire and the expertise necessary to restrict to a minimum the damage caused by transfers.

There is, however, a sense in which the operation of Water Authorities in maintaining water quality could be described as a little narrow. Consents on discharges to river and sewer often force manufacturers to instal their own treatment plants. In cases where a particular type of waste is most easily treated without mixing, then this may be the most efficient solution. Where, however, the consent is imposed to restrict the toxicity of a sludge resulting from treatment, it may be that it would be more efficient in the long run for the Water Authority to undertake the full treatment, making the full charge for the task. Since the waterborne environment may be threatened by sludge with a high metal content, it would seem safer (if not cheaper) to have the authority responsible for water quality dispose of it. The opinion of the Water Authority concerning, for example, the safety of disposing of sludge agriculturally would seem to be in many instances better informed than the opinion of the firm involved. We suspect that there are other cases, where strict consent conditions are currently imposed on a particular kind of waste, but where it would be safer and/or cheaper for any additional treatment to be undertaken by those best qualified to judge the environmental effects of residuals arising from treatment.

Of course, much of the field of environmental management is currently in a transitional period pending the full implementation of the Control of Pollution Act. When this process is complete, the framework for pollution control will allow Water Authorities more comprehensive jurisdiction over tidal waters and tips. It is our opinion that, given their existing expertise, the Authorities will be in a good position to restrict transfers of pollution to a desirable level in the future.

Our discussions revealed that air-water transfers of pollution from industrial processes were not as extensive as we had initially been led to believe. Of those that do arise, the use of wet scrubbing devices in iron and steel manufacture are amongst the commonest. The potential for water-solid transfers from tipping was considered to be more serious by representatives that we spoke to; and of wastes tipped that arising from the Metal Finishing Industry is amongst the most toxic.

REFERENCES

1. Julian Lowe and David Lewis. 'The Economics of Environmental Management'. Philip Allen, 1980

CHAPTER 3

The Fertilizer Industry

INTRODUCTION

The fertilizer industry includes the production of the basic inorganic chemicals, ammonia, sulphuric, phosphoric and nitric acids, although these are not fertilizers in themselves. In general there are two categories of fertilizer plant; large integrated complexes and small mixer plants. The former produce the basic chemicals which are necessary for the manufacture of all the various types of fertilizer as well as some of these fertilizers themselves. The latter receive all their raw materials from the large complexes and carry out only those mixing operations that are required.

The three essential plant nutrients - Nitrogen (N), Phosphorous (P) and Potassium (K) - form the essential "building blocks" of the industry. Industry jargon identifies two types of product - "straight" and "compound" fertilizers. The former consists of only a single nutrient and the latter is defined as one containing two or more primary plant nutrients. In turn, these can be classified as being either of the "mixed" or "blended" type (fertilizers obtained by mixing nutrients without any subsequent chemical reaction) or the "complex" type (fertilizers obtained by chemical reactions with or without agglomeration as a preceding step. Much of the mixed fertilizer is granulated whereby it is formed into small spherical agglomerations of 0.25 - 0.5 cm diameter or it is prilled whereby it is formed into small spherical beads varying from 0.1 - 0.2 cm in diameter.

For most fertilizer products, the production process can be divided into wet and dry parts. The chemical reactions which constitute the major part of the production process are generally referred to as the wet part. In most cases the final product is in a solid form and consequently there is a dry part consisting of various mechanical operations such as prilling or granulating, drying, cooling, conveying and bagging. The various dry operations can be combined with any wet unit process. For many fertilizer products the production process is a complicated chain of (wet) unit processes and (dry) operations.

The raw materials, principally Phosphorous (as raw phosphates), Potassium (as potash) and Nitrogen (as air), are converted into mainly soluble

forms that can be used by plants. Basically, this is done by transforming
atmospheric nitrogen into ammonia and causing phosphate ore to react with
sulphuric and phosphoric acids. Other nutrients are often added during
production, with or without intention. The relationships between the
various raw materials, basic chemicals and fertilizer products are shown
in Figure 3.I

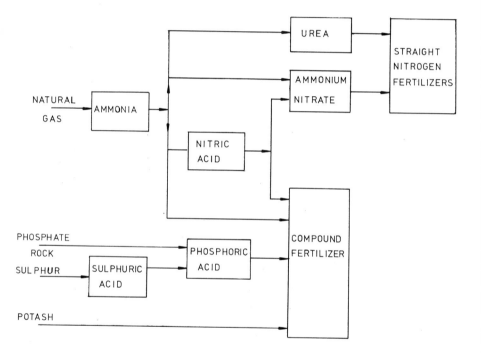

Fig 3.I. Simplified fertilizer production flowsheet

SOURCES OF CROSS-MEDIA TRANSFERS

The manufacture of <u>ammonia</u> causes relatively few pollution problems.
However, there are three areas where potential cross-media transfers occur.

I. <u>Condensation Units</u> — in this instance the gas stream is condensed
to liquid, i.e. there is an air to water pollution transfer. However,
the condensation units are more properly to be regarded as part of
the production process rather than part of environmental control.

2. Purge gases - these can be scrubbed thus creating an air to water pollution transfer. However, the ammonia in the effluent is too valuable to be allowed to escape so it is usually recovered and accordingly no environmental trade-offs arise.

3. Process condensate - this can be fed to a stripping tower to remove volatile gases such as ammonia and carbon dioxide, i.e. there is a water to air pollution transfer. This can be considered as a secondary cross-media transfer (water to air) since the primary transfer (air to water) occurs at the condensation units; as these transfers arise out of the need to control atmospheric emission, it seems reasonable to suppose that environmental trade-offs do arise in this instance.

The major source of emissions from sulphuric acid manufacture is the tail gas from the absorption tower. Cross-media transfers can result from the scrubbing of the tail gases, i.e. air to water pollution transfers. However, in most cases the companies involved arrange matters so that either the by-products are re-cycled or that they can be sold. An exceptional case is when lime slurry is used as the scrubbing medium as in this case the resulting calcium sulphate/sulphite sludge has to be disposed of. This is, therefore, an air to water transfer (or, if the sludge is greater than 10 per cent solids, an air to solids transfer) and environmental trade-offs do arise. This sludge can cause secondary cross-media transfers in the form of surface water run-off and leaching at the dumping ground if adequate steps are not taken to prevent them. Pollution problems may also occur during the transfer of the sludge to the dumping ground which are generated by the transport vehicle:

> noxious fumes from the lorry exhaust
> lorry noise
> vibrations due to lorry passage
> accidents and/or spillages
> congestion of roads

Clearly, the extent to which these factors are important depends, in part, on the number of vehicle movements involved.

Pollution from nitric acid manufacture is mainly due to nitric acid absorption tower tail gases. Potential cross-media transfers can result from wet scrubbing (i.e. air to water transfers). However, as with sulphuric acid plant tail gases, it is usually arranged for the by-product to be re-cycled or sold and it seems reasonable to suppose that environmental trade-offs do not arise here.

Intra-media transfers can arise due to the incineration or catalytic reduction of the tail gases. In such cases an invisible plume is produced where the emissions have only been converted from a visible to an invisible form. This method of "pollution control" may also generate other additional pollutants (such as sulphur dioxide or carbon monoxide) as a result of the combustion processes involved.

Phosphoric acid manufacture provides several examples of cross-media transfers of pollution. These result mainly from the removal of dust and fluorine-containing gases and also in the disposal of the gypsum by-product.

1. Fluorine removal - various types of wet scrubbing equipment can
be used thus causing an air to water pollution transfer and trade-off.
In many cases, however, the fluorine is recovered for re-cycle or sale.
There is also considerable general re-use of water within plants.

2. Dust removal - wet scrubbing equipment can also be used to control
the dust problem thus causing an air to water pollution transfer and
trade-off. If bag filters are employed there is an air to solid transfer
of pollution but no trade-off if the captured material is re-used;
alternatively it may be disposed of together with the gypsum sludge.

3. Gypsum disposal - in most methods of disposal there are no direct
cross-media pollution transfers and much gypsum disposal takes place
at sea. However, secondary cross-media transfers may arise if the
gypsum is disposed of in a lagoon; in particular, this may cause dust
problems (i.e. a solid to air transfer) when the lagoon has dried out.
The lagoon may also produce problems arising from surface run-off and
leachate if adequate steps are not taken to prevent it.

Significant cross-media pollution transfers result from the manufacture
of urea.

1. Dust and fume removal - approximately 0.2% of daily production may be
lost as ammonia and urea fumes and there are various scrubbing methods for
the removal of these at the prilling tower. These will create a liquid
effluent, the nature of which will depend upon the scrubbing medium. Many
urea prilling towers employ an impinger type device with a baffle plate
and a water curtain system but the effectiveness of such a system is in
doubt. However, sulphuric acid may also be used as the scrubbing medium
and in this case the ammonium sulphate by-product must be disposed of
(there is no market for it) and an environmental trade-off will arise.
Where cyclone units are installed to trap dust there will be an air to
solid pollution transfer.

Another solution to the inter-media trade-off problem would consist of a
hydrolyzer stripper system. This would be considered to constitute
pollution control rather than materials recovery as the amount of product
recovered and consequent economic advantage to any firm adopting it would
seem to be low. In this system the urea is first hydrolyzed to ammonia
which is then stripped out. In this way ammonia and urea losses can be
reduced and the effluent from the stripping unit re-cycled; however there
would be a minor emission of ammonia. Ammonia could also be released from
the hydrolysis of urea in a concentrator and this give rise to ammonia in
the crystalliser condensate.

It is understood that some manufacturers have ceased prilling urea and have
changed over to granulation or spheroidisation processes in view of the
cost of abatement on existing prill towers.

2. Water pollution control - stripping liquid effluents which arise in
urea plants from crystalliser condensate, purge gas scrubbing liquors and
prill tower dust control apparatus and contains ammonia and urea will
cause air to air pollution transfer. This can be considered as secondary
transfer as the liquid effluent may be generated by scrubbing equipment
in the first instance.

Lagooning the effluent may cause a water to air pollution transfer as ammonia will be gradually evolved. It may also be considered an environmental trade-off since unpleasant odours may be generated. Where biological methods are used to control the liquid effluent from a urea plant there may be secondary and tertiary pollution transfers. The biological methods usually create a sludge which will create pollution problems when it is transported to the dumping ground as well as run-off and leachate problems at the tip.

Similar cross-media transfers arise in ammonium nitrate manufacture.

1. Dust and fume removal - in the ammonium nitrate prilling tower (as in the urea prilling tower) there is an air to water pollution transfer. However, in ammonium nitrate manufacture there are also gaseous emissions from the neutraliser unit. Air to water transfers occur when these emissions are condensed or when they are scrubbed. The extent to which trade-offs arise will depend upon the extent to which the resulting liquors can be re-used within the plant.

The evolution of both ammonia and fume from the prilling tower depends upon the melt pH and temperature, and the rate of cooling. The optimum pH can be calculated at which the total loss (in terms of nitrogen) is minimised. This is a pH of about 6.5 but operations may be carried out at higher pH in order to give a less visible plume at the expense of ammonia losses and poorer product quality. An ordinary wet scrubber installed on an ammonium nitrate prilling tower would not have very much effect on the ammonium nitrate fume generated and may produce a wet, steamy plume in cold weather which would be a return to the amenity problem. In part the emissions can be partially reduced by building an extra tall tower which operates with lower air velocities thereby reducing the emission of dust and mini-prills, but this does not affect fume formation.

2. Water pollution control - again the same type of cross-media pollution transfers occur here as in urea manufacture, that is, water to air secondary pollution transfers resulting from stripping the effluent, water to air pollution transfers from lagooning and secondary and tertiary pollution transfers from biological treatment. However, liquid effluent streams are often re-cycled or sold as liquid fertilizer so the problem can be minimised and few trade-offs arise.

Losses can be minimised by good pH control and by a carefully designed and operated system, which allows effluent to be re-cycled and re-used within the plant. This is unlikely to lead to any perceptible reduction in production quality. Although relatively minor problems may arise in some cases, these are not in terms of impurities that become incorporated in the fertilizer products.

Two sources of air to water transfers may be identified as arising in ammonium phosphate manufacture.

1. Ammonia removal from gaseous emissions - ammonia gases are usually scrubbed but because of the amount of re-cycling involved in these plants there is only a limited air to water transfer and trade-offs do not arise. Fluorine removal from gaseous emissions - Fluorine-containing gases are usually scrubbed and, as with ammonia control, because of the amount of re-cycling involved the air to water pollution transfers cause very few

problems and again trade-offs do not arise. There is a tendency in ammonium phosphate processes to form sludge from the combined wastes. The cross-media pollution transfers and trade-offs involved with sludge generation and disposal are the same as those discussed in the sections on sulphuric acid and urea.

2. Water pollution control - aqueous effluents are sometimes treated with lime thus generating a sludge problem with corresponding secondary and tertiary transfers similar to those already discussed in the sections on sulphuric acid and urea manufacture.

The cross-media pollution problems in superphosphate manufacture are also similar to those found in phosphoric acid and ammonium phosphate manufacture. Wet-scrubbing to remove fluorine and dust will cause an air to water pollution transfer and trade-off. However, fluorine is often recovered or alternatively the water is recycled so that few problems arise from this cross-media pollution transfer. Where bag filters or cyclones are used to control dust there will be an air to solid transfer. Secondary and tertiary transfers and trade-offs may occur depending on how this solid residue is disposed of. It may be tipped directly or with a sludge generated within the process; in these cases the other cross-media transfers and pollution problems are the same as those described in the sections on sludge in sulphuric acid and urea manufacture.

The "dry" parts of fertilizer production processes have serious pollution potential.

1. Ammonia and fluorine fumes are generally controlled by wet scrubbing, thus causing air to water transfer. However, liquid effluent streams are often re-cycled or used as liquid fertilizers so trade-offs are minimal.

2. Dust is usually controlled by bag filters and/or cyclones thus causing an air to solid transfer. Secondary and tertiary pollution transfers may occur as described in earlier sections on urea and sulphuric acid. Dust can also be controlled by wet scrubbing methods, e.g. spray or wash towers are often employed, and in these cases there will be an air to water pollution transfer and trade-off. Sludges are commonly formed by combining the aqueous effluent streams and the cross-media transfers and pollution problems so created have been discussed in the sections on sulphuric acid and urea manufacture.

CASE STUDIES OF FERTILIZER MANUFACTURERS*

As has already been explained, the nature of fertilizer manufacturers is that typically they are multi-product enterprises and to follow the normal pattern of case-study reporting by presenting in sequence all information

---

* The following case studies are based upon information supplied by four fertilizer manufacturers and by two firms of specialist consultants who were able to supply data based upon previously published information. We are grateful to the firms involved for their permission to publish the information about them and for giving their time in assisting the study. We have not named them in order to help preserve an element of confidentiality.

for every firm would almost certainly be confusing in this instance.
Instead, we have chosen to arrange the case information in product sequence,
for the four major products and for dry processes. In part, of course, this
helps to retain the anonymity of the cases but this was not the primary
purpose.

Firm I is a large scale manufacturer of a variety of fertilizers; sources
of cross-media transfers are few at its plant but it is interesting to note
that the particular type of production technology employed results in very
low emission rates. Firm 2 produces ammonia, ammonium nitrate, nitric acid
and compound fertilizers; significant environmental trade-offs arise at
this plant and at the insistence of the Water Authority an effluent
treatment plant was built at a cost of £2m. Firm 3 is another large company
operating an integrated complex producing phosphoric acid and nitric acid
among other products. Firm 4 is a typical small fertilizer manufacturing
company which mixes compound fertilizers and where the principal environmental trade-off arises through the use of a wet scrubber to control
emissions of fertilizer dust from the bagging plant.

Environmental Considerations in Nitric Acid Manufacture*

The tail gas from a nitric acid plant consists of a small amount of water
vapour (about 0.6%), some oxygen (between 2 and 3%), nitric oxide and
nitrogen dioxide gases (at most 0.2 or 0.3%) and the remainder (in excess
of 95%) nitrogen. The emissions of concern are the nitrogen oxides as they
contribute to nitrates in the fallout from the plant and because the
nitrogen dioxide is orange coloured. The volume of tail gases is large,
approximately 33,000Nm³/hr (about 41 tonnes/hr) for a plant with an output
of 250 tonnes per day of nitric acid. The 1979 standards of control
applied to new plants in the U.K. by the Alkali Inspectorate were such
that NO_x emissions had to be below 1000 ppm and be colourless; for
practical purposes an emission rate of 200 ppm would be accepted as being
colourless. Thus, providing a stack emission could be "cosmetically"
rendered colourless, an emission rate of up to 1000 ppm NO_x would be
acceptable.

Two types of nitric acid plant may be constructed: "single" or "dual"
pressure plants. Single pressure plants, operating in the range of 5-9
atmospheres, will obtain NO_x emission rates of typically 1,000 to 3,000 ppm
and, with further treatment, could achieve 200 ppm. Alternatively a
"dual" pressure plant may be constructed to directly achieve the required
emission rate of 200 ppm although this is less efficient in the sense that
the capital cost of the plant is higher (an additional compressor is
required) and less steam (up to 0.3 tonnes/tonne of product) is available
for export. Catalyst consumption and ammonia conversion efficiency is
good - similar to 5 atmospheres and better than 9 atmospheres single
pressure plants (by slightly less than 2 per cent). Further, more pumps
are required and an additional energy requirement of 3 Kwh/tonne
(10.8×10^6 Joules) is needed. Thus, whilst the dual pressure plant has
environmental advantages in that no end-of-line pollution control is

---

* This information was largely supplied by Humphreys and Glasgow Ltd.
Contracting Engineers. We are grateful to them for giving their time and
supplying the data.

TABLE 3.1 Nitric Acid Tail Gas Abatement Systems

Process Type	Additional absorption	Additional absorption (Catalyst-aided)	Molecular sieve adsorption	Catalytic reduction with fuel	Catalytic reduction with ammonia	Ammonia scrubbing
Process name	"Extended absorption"	CDL/Vitok	"Purasiv N"		NO/NOx	Goodpasture
Developer	Soc.Chimique de la Grand Paroisse (France)	Chenoweth Development Labs.Vitok Engineers (U.S.A.)	Union Carbide (U.S.A.)		Gulf Oil Chemicals (U.S.A.)	Goodpasture Inc (U.S.A.)
Type of installation	Modification to main plant	"Bolt-on" retrofit	"Bolt-on" retrofit	"Bolt-on" retrofit	"Bolt-on" retrofit	"Bolt-on" retrofit
Credits	Extra HNO_3	Extra HNO_3	Extra HNO_3	Steam		Ammonium nitrate
Size of main acid plant	360 stpd 300 stpd	200 stpd	55 stpd	300 stpd	300 stpd	100 stpd
Volume of tail gas	33,000 scfm	17,500 scfm	4,700 scfm			8,500 scfm
NO_x concentration (as NO_2)	2,500 ppmv	4,000 ppmv	3,000 ppmv			2,000-5,000 ppmv
Exit NO_x (as NO_2)	180 ppmv	200 ppmv	50 ppmv		200 ppmv	150 - 200 ppmv
Reference date	1973 1978	1975/76	1975	1978	1978	1976
Capital cost at ref. date	$0.55m $1.16m	$450,000	$375,000	$1.6 million	$38,000	$200,000
Utilities per s. ton HNO_3:						
Electricity	0.82 kWh	2.13 kWh	35.3 kWh			
Steam	-	57 lb	62.9 lb			
Fuel	-	-	-			
Ammonia					0.01 s.ton	
Cooling water	1,200 galls (US)	4,900 US gallons	2,475 US gallons			
Net abatement cost per s.ton HNO_3	$0.05 $3.25* (0.63)*	$3.20 (4.65)*		$6.85*	$2.30*	$0.25

*Data on a comparable basis but may refer to different years

required, it has some operating disadvantages and a single pressure
plant with suitable controls may prove an acceptable and more economical
alternative. Costs of control at some sites are presented in Table 3.1.

Controls suitable for single pressure plants - These may be considered
as end-of-line pollution control devices except for (4). Their objectives
are to reduce NO_x emissions or reduce colour, or both.

1. Catalytic combustion

   (i) using a hydrocarbon fuel (such as natural gas, naphtha, hydrogen,
                               or ammonia plant purge gas)

This may be used to convert the nitrogen dioxide to nitric oxide (thereby
rendering the tail gas invisible but not altering the total NO_x emission)
or it may also be used to reduce total NO_x emissions to a level of 200 ppm
by conversion of nitric oxide to nitrogen. In practice it is found that
about half the stoichiometric amount of fuel required to reduce the total
NO_x to nitrogen, is required to render the tail gas colourless without
affecting the total NO_x emitted. Thereafter additional fuel produces an
increasing reduction in the NO_x concentration until a limit of 50 to 200 ppm
is reached. Accordingly, it requires only twice as much fuel to reduce
total NO_x to 200 ppm as it does to reduce the emission to a colourless
state. Whilst there is an increase in fuel usage (300 mega/calories/tonne
HNO_3 are required for reduction of total NO_x to 200 ppm) it is possible
that an additional 0.65 tonnes of steam/tonne HNO_3 would be available for
recovery and use elsewhere on the site. In some plants it may be possible
that suitable fuel is available on site (particularly in the form of
ammonia plant purge gas) and the ability to use this may, in fact, result
in an overall increase in the operating efficiency of the plant.

Whilst the rate of consumption of acid production catalyst will remain
unchanged in a plant fitted with a catalytic combustion system, it may be
necessary to use sulphur resistant catalysts or a low sulphur content fuel.
Depending on the sulphur content of the fuel which would control SO_2
emissions, final emissions would be 200 ppm NO_x, some unburnt hydrocarbons
and ammonia, both of the order of 10 ppm. Towards the end of the catalyst's
life, greater NO_x slip is experienced with a certain amount of incomplete
combustion of the fuel which may require extra care in design and operation
to maintain standards.

   (ii) using ammonia

This process - which has not yet been adopted in the U.K. - uses ammonia to
react with NO_x gases over a catalyst. The rate of ammonia consumption of
the plant would be increased slightly (probably by no more than 1 per cent)
and NO_x emissions could be reduced to 200 ppm. The additional energy input

required for such control plant would be very small indeed and only relate
to that needed to overcome the pressure drop over the catalyst. There
would be no recovery opportunities, however, and the tail gas emissions
would contain up to 200 ppm ammonia.

2. Scrubbing with caustic soda or urea

Another system for control of NO_x emissions uses caustic soda or urea as
a scrubbing medium for fume; this generates a potential cross-media
transfer since the sodium nitrate/nitrite or ammonium nitrite solutions
resulting would require to be treated since discharge to a water-course
may not be permitted. In most cases it would be desirable to recover
these solutions and make them available for re-use or re-sale. If this
were not possible an environmental trade-off would arise.

3. Additional dilution

Providing the NO_x limit of 1000 ppm is achieved, it is clear that any
measures to render the fume colourless would be acceptable and it is
possible to achieve this by greater dilution. A definition of colourlessness in common use is that a stack emission will be colourless if the NO_2
concentration in ppm is less than

$$\frac{2400}{\text{diameter of stack in inches}}$$

Increasing the dilution (and keeping stack velocity constant) would
require an increase in stack diameter; a 1:1 dilution would require an
approximate 40% increase in stack diameter. This will help achieve
colourlessness but the effect would be marginal. For example, a stack
30 inches diameter would need NO_2 emissions to be below 80 ppm for
invisibility. An initial emission of 100 ppm would not be considered
colourless but by arranging for 1:1 dilution the concentration would fall
to 50 ppm. An increase in stack diameter would be needed from 30 to
42 inches and the lower limit for colourlessness would be slightly below
60 ppm which would be achieved. Increased dilution can only be achieved
at the expense of slightly increased energy input (needed to drive the
extra gas up the stack) and accordingly the environmental benefits are
not unequivocal.

4. Improved absorption

A further method of reducing emissions, really applicable to high pressure
plants only is to modify the plant to pass tail gases through an additional
absorber. By this means, emissions of 2000 ppm would be reduced to 200 ppm
with a concomitant increase in acid production (every 1000 ppm of NO_x
emission represents 1% acid loss). However, it will be appreciated that
the capital cost is high and the amount of acid gain is low; further, the
energy requirement rises because of the increased pressure drop and the
export of energy from the plant may fall by as much as 10%. This method
has not yet been adopted in the U.K. although, of course, it is implicitly
the method adopted in mixed pressure plants.

5. Molecular sieves

These have been proposed for use on nitric acid plants but as yet they can
only be considered to be in the experimental stage.

The Nitric Acid Plant at Firm I

Ammonia is delivered to the plant by rail or coastal tanker and is
discharged from a temporary holding tank into a storage sphere of 700
tonnes capacity both at about 5°C and 60 p.s.i.g. Elaborate safety
precautions are taken over the discharge of the rail wagons and of the
conduct of the whole ammonia operation. From the main storage sphere, the
ammonia passes to a warm water heated vapouriser and thence to the ammonium
nitrate plant and to the nitric acid plant. In the latter it is mixed
with air at high pressure (provided by steam turbine) and thence over a
platinum gauze catalyst. After filtration and cooling, the gases pass to
the absorber tower where they are mixed with condensate process water which
originates from the prill plant. The gases to the absorption tower are
water cooled (approximately 700m³/hr of water are used) and, after
absorption, recirculation and bleaching, approximately 15 tons per hour
of 55/60% nitric acid are produced. Gas emissions from the absorber tower
pass to the stack (which is approximately 66m high) via a heat exchanger
and a turbine. Approximately 28,000m³/hr (equivalent to 34 tonnes/hr) of
gas are emitted; the plant consistently operates at between 1,200 ppm and
2,000 ppm – well within the limit of 2,700 ppm extant at the time of our
visit. Even so, at these concentrations the fume is clearly visible, and
is especially noticeable at times when the plant is starting up.

Environmental Considerations in Sulphuric Acid Manufacture

In sulphuric acid plants a catalytic reactor is used to oxidise sulphur
dioxide to sulphur trioxide which is then absorbed in 98-99% sulphuric
acid to make more acid. The unabsorbed tail gas is exhausted to atmosphere;
this contains largely oxygen and nitrogen but details on other pollutants
are shown in Table 3.3. The tail gas may also contain a sulphuric acid

TABLE 3.3   Concentration of pollutants in sulphuric acid
            plant tail gas

	Concentration (ppmv)
Sulphur dioxide	200 – 4,000
Sulphur trioxide	0 – 100
Sulphuric acid vapour	250 – 1,000
Sulphuric acid mist	10 – 500
Nitrogen oxides	0 – 200

mist which, although not concentrated, is the most visible of the pollutants. There are two alternative paths to pollution control; increased absorption of sulphur dioxide to produce more acid and tail gas scrubbing using liquid or solid adsorbents. An interesting external benefit may, in fact, arise for those sulphuric acid plants which are located close to power plants which use sulphur recovery since, by using the same recovery process in the sulphuric acid plant as at the power plant, overall costs to both parties may be reduced.

Increased absorption, of which there are several methods, can largely be ignored for present purposes since there are few, if any, environmental trade-offs. A small plant with 132 t.p.d. capacity would have a power requirement of 4KW (presumably per ton of acid) and an unspecified amount of sludge to be disposed of. No other residuals are likely to be produced by these control methods except in the case of a method using an irrigated carbon catalyst when only weak acid can be produced which may have to be disposed of thus creating an inter-media trade-off.

On the other hand, processes which absorb the sulphur dioxide in liquid or solid absorbents are possible and may lead to substantial trade-offs; further, such processes require substantial amounts of heat to regenerate the absorbent which will clearly affect the economics as well as the overall pollution balance of the system. Tail gas scrubbing with lime will produce calcium sulphite and sulphate which may either be dumped at sea or disposed of on a tip. A similar end product arises if the tail gas is scrubbed with sodium hydroxide solution. In some cases, sodium sulphate may be generated as a waste product to be disposed of as a solution. With the use of solid adsorbents, it has been suggested that lower emission levels may be achievable than with other materials and difficulties over disposal of secondary residuals have not been reported.

As has already been stated, sulphuric acid mist is a highly visible pollutant that may be emitted by sulphuric acid plants. This mist may be controlled in various ways (scrubbing with an aqueous solution is unlikely to be of any use and may make matters worse); venturi scrubbers may be used with the main drawback that a high power consumption is reported; electrostatic precipitators may also be used and so also may filters of various types. Residuals from these items of equipment would not be expected to present important environmental trade-offs.

Sulphuric Acid Production at Firm I

The design of the sulphuric acid plant dates from about 20 years ago and uses the Monsanto contact process. The plant has a capacity of 50 tonnes per day and discharges 6,200m³/hr of gas (containing 0.7 - 1.5 grains/ft³ SO_3; the presumptive limit is 4 grains/ft³) through a stack 36m high. There are no liquid effluent discharges from this plant except for towns water which has passed externally over a cooling cascade. The company indicated that, despite its small size in comparison with the rest of the works, the sulphuric acid plant was perhaps the single most important source of complaints (which are, in any case, few) and this arises because sulphuric acid droplets can be emitted from the stack when the plant is starting up (although this only occurs about once a year). This problem is severe only when the wind blows in a particular direction and the management tries to avoid starting up at that time.

Environmental Considerations in Ammonium Nitrate Manufacture

Ammonium nitrate has to be at or above its melting point for prilling. Because the reaction by which ammonium nitrate is formed is in equilibrium, there is an appreciable vapour pressure of ammonia and nitric acid over it at this sort of temperature. These gases tend to be carried out of the plant in the vapours from the neutralizer, evaporator and in the prill tower cooling air. When they cool, they recombine to form a blue fog of very minute ammonium nitrate particles - much too small to be arrested in any physical dust removal system such as a bag filter.

This fume is the principal problem in ammonium nitrate plants, and it is a difficulty owing to the very large volume of air which passes through the prill tower. For example, the air flow through a prill tower for a 150 t.p.d. ammonium nitrate plant may be as much as 120,000 s.c.f.m, containing perhaps 100-150 mg ammonium nitrate fume per cubic metre.

Because of the large air volumes, it is not a practical proposition to remove ammonium nitrate fume by conventional scrubbing or filtering. The fume particles are of such a small size as to demand an efficiency of the scrubbing or filtering device which would impose a very large pressure drop and consequently consume an enormous amount of energy.

The ammonium nitrate fume control system developed by one American company uses fibre bed filters to capture fume particles from exhaust air from the neutralizer, evaporator and prill tower. The key to the process is a conical shroud around the prilling head which deflects only the air that comes into contact with the solidfying hot ammonium nitrate droplets into the filtering system, allowing the majority of the prill tower air (which comes into contact only with the cooler prills and, therefore, contains very little fume) to escape untreated to the atmosphere. The remaining air is combined with relatively small flows of vapours from the neutralizer and evaporator and is passed through an assembly of irrigated mist eliminator elements. The initial ones are designed to trap larger particles of dust from broken product; the subsequent elements are of the "high-efficiency" kind and remove micron-sized particles.

This system is capable of reducing emissions from a typical rate of 4 lb per ton to 1 lb per ton - well below the U.S. Environmental Protection Agency's limit of about 1.4 lb per ton. Opacity is typically 10-20% corresponding to a particulate loading of 0.006 - 0.012 grains per cu.ft. (0.013 - 0.026 g per Nm³). Given that is is possible that such a system may be undertaken for economic rather than environmental reasons, it is impossible to be certain about the existence of environmental trade-offs.

Alternatively, a substantial reduction in ammonium nitrate emissions from "high-velocity" prill towers can be achieved by reducing the velocity of the air up the tower, as a proportion of the solid material emitted is in the form of microprills. On the other hand, reducing the air velocity will reduce the capacity of the tower. This problem was solved in a 500 s.t.p.d. prilling installation in Canada by replacing a nozzle-plate at the top of the tower by two spray heads, each enclosed in a metal shroud and open only at its lower end. In this way, the hot prill droplets start their fall (where ammonia vapour losses and microprill entrainment are normally at their worst) through still air.

Despite an increase in air flow rate and velocity in the body of the tower, which more than compensated for the loss of cooling in the space enclosed

by the shroud, and which, therefore, enabled the throughput of the tower
to be raised, this expedient reduced ammonium nitrate losses from the
tower from 15.7 lbs per ton to 2.87 lbs per ton and ammonia vapour losses
from 0.43 lbs per ton to 0.25 lbs per ton. The air flow was boosted from
265,000 c.f.m. to 550,000 c.f.m. The capital cost of the modifications
(reported in late 1975) was $25,000. Apart from the additional power
needed to drive the fans, which in this case is at least partly down to
the expansion in capacity, no additional utility consumption is involved
and the environmental trade-offs involved are probably only slight.

The Ammonium Nitrate Plant at Firm I

There are two plants for producing ammonium nitrate solution, each of
500 TPD capacity on this site, but at the time of our visit the company
was proposing to build a third plant of 650 TPD capacity. Anhydrous
gaseous ammonia is neutralised with 58% nitric acid in these plants to
produce ammonium nitrate. This is an exothermic reaction and the heat is
used to concentrate the ammonium nitrate solution to 98%.

There are four sources of emission from these plants - the neutraliser, the
evaporator, the prilling tower and the cooler. Heavy losses occur at the
neutraliser but atmospheric pollution is avoided at this source by
condensing the large quantities of steam (containing ammonium nitrate and
ammonia) produced in the reaction. This, however, occurs at the expense
of creating an aqueous effluent which was discharged to a canal.

Of the remaining three sources, all of which cause atmospheric pollution,
that from the prilling tower is most serious. There are no controls on
the prilling towers to abate the gaseous emissions which can cause a serious
amenity problem. Contained in the, sometimes dense, blue/grey emissions
are ammonia, ammonium nitrate mini-prills and ammonium nitrate fume. It
has been said that emissions have laid waste to 6-8 acres of land around
the complex, mainly due to the ammonium nitrate falling on the vegetation
and causing scorching on the leaves and general plant damage. At one
stage suggestions had been made to the firm that these emissions could
cause methaemoglobinemia and gastric cancers but a medical expert called in
by the company showed this was not the case.

Because of the effluent restriction imposed on the company by the Water
Authority (and in line with the company's own phase 2 expansion) an
effluent treatment plant to deal with the liquid effluents was under
construction at the time of our visit. This plant would take the dilute
ammonium nitrate stream from the condensers, decompose the ammonium nitrate
and recover the ammonia. However, half a tonne of steam would be required
to decompose each tonne of the dilute ammonium nitrate stream and only a
1% ammonium solution recovered. Because of the costs involved and the
uneconomical situation (as far as the company is concerned) the plant would
never have been built unless it had been required by the Water Authority.
It was estimated to cost £2m, but it would also take the wastes from the
proposed 650 TPD ammonium nitrate plant and keep the effluent within the
restrictions imposed.

Ammonium Nitrate and Compound Fertilizer Prilling Plants at Firm 2

Within the present context, it is sensible to discuss both these plants together since they both utilise, in this case, the one important potential source of atmospheric emissions - the prill tower. As it turns out, the prill plant is also the most important source of liquid discharges from the site, accounting for all the nitrate, 90% of the ammonia, 90% of the phosphoric acid and 90% of the potassium discharges. The liquid effluent is mainly derived from slightly contaminated condensates from various evaporation stages of the ammonium nitrate and/or ammonium phosphate concentration process.

Gas from the first stage evaporator on the ammonium nitrate solution plant is scrubbed before discharge in order to recover ammonia. Similarly, gas from the second stage ammonium nitrate evaporator (which is located at the top of the prill tower) is also scrubbed to recover ammonia. The company would not describe these scrubbers as pollution control but would rather see these as materials recovery as they are essential to the economic viability of the plant.

Because of the large volumes of gas involved, the prill tower is the single most important potential source of atmospheric emissions but tests conducted on it when making ammonium nitrate showed that emissions of ammonia were about 3.1 kg/hr (7lb/hr) and emissions of nitrate about 0.32 kg/hr (0.72 lb/hr); this from a plant with a productive capacity of 15/25 tonnes/hr. These emissions would be entrained in approximately 340,000m³/hr (405 tonnes/hr) of air drawn up through the tower and discharged roughly two thirds of the way up the tower at a height of 50m (these figures are the raw residual loads and not post-control loads). The concentration is approximately 0.001gm/m³.

The height of the prill tower was chosen for production rather than environmental considerations, the critical factor being that the molten droplets must solidify before they reach the bottom. However, although there is a discharge of a faint white haze mostly consisting of water droplets condensed on ammonium nitrate nuclei when this product is being made, emissions are virtually invisible when compound fertilizers are being produced because of the unique design of the prill tower which itself is a consequence of the firm's desire to prill compounds. Thus, a production design has a significant (and beneficial) bearing upon environmental impact.

Environmental Consideration in Phosphoric Acid Manufacture - Firm 3

There are two phosphoric acid plants within the complex. One is of the Dorr-Oliver type. Both types employ basically the same manufacturing process and the differences between the plants lie in the configuration and methods of cooling. These differences in turn affect the levels of gaseous emissions and liquid effluents, although the combined gaseous and aqueous emissions will be similar.

The dihydrate process of these plants involves the reaction of phosphate rock and sulphuric acid in a series or "train" of agitated reactor tanks through which the slurry cascades by gravity. The retention time in the system ranges from 4 to 8 hours. The initial step consists of pre-mixing sulphuric acid with recycled weak phosphoric acid and recirculated slurry to produce about 3% free sulphuric acid. Dry, ground rock is added to this mixture in slightly less than the stoichiometric proportion required

for complete reaction, to maintain a slight excess of sulphuric acid in
the system. The slurry then flows through successive reactor tanks in
which the temperature and acid concentration are controlled to ensure
completeness of reaction and growth of gypsum crystals to the size necessary
for effecting good separation of acid and gypsum in the filtration stage.
The constant addition of acid causes an overflow of slurry from which
phosphoric acid is extracted through a filter.

In effect, after leaving the last reactor tank, the slurry is split into
two streams in a ratio of about 15 to 1. The larger stream is recirculated
to the pre-mixing tank to be intermixed with fresh sulphuric acid (96-98%);
the slurry is pumped to the filter for separation and washing of the gypsum
crystals. The filter operation involves three continuous stages. The
product acid, containing 28-32% P_2O_5, is separated from the gypsum in the
first stage, and the phosphoric acid remaining is washed from the gypsum
residue during the second and third stages. Industrial fresh water is used
to wash the gypsum at the third stage; the filtrate from this is circulated
over the gypsum in the second stage, where the acid concentration reaches
about 20% P_2O_5, and is then pumped back into the pre-mixing tank. The
waste gypsum is slurried in sea water and discharged. The product acid
from the filter is concentrated in an evaporator to a strength of 48-49%
P_2O_5, because the 28-32% P_2O_5 strength originally produced is too weak for
commercial purposes.

Emission control - Plant 1

The gases evolved during the previously described production process (in
particular from the reactors and acid concentrators) contain fluorine as
HF and SiF_4. They are drawn off into two wash towers which employ a water
spray. The spray scrubs out the fluorides. The operating efficiency
(based on phosphoric acid scrubbing efficiency) of a wash tower is 95% or
more. It has not yet proved possible to assess accurately fluorine recovery
efficiency. The effluent from a wash tower is variable but contains about
50 kg/hr and 10 kg/hr of fluorine and dilute phosphoric acid (as P_2O_5),
respectively.

Matters are complicated by the fact that in order to save water, part of
that used within the plants is recycled. The dock water used to condense
the steam evolved in the acid evaporators contains a proportion of fluorine.
Part of this dock water is then used to wash the gases in the wash tower
and part is used to slurry the gypsum. Eventually, both streams are
combined in the effluent. The fluorine compounds contained in the effluent
from the wash towers amount to approximately 200 kg/hr at a concentration
of approximately 2,000 ppm.

Cross media transfers of pollution

For some time this company has been studying the fluorine emissions from
its plant and these studies have been conducted in consultation with various
government departments. Considerable difficulties have been encountered in
developing a sampling system which is adequate for the sampling of
gas/droplet streams, from wet scrubbed stacks. Whilst gaseous emissions
are important, the evidence suggests that the majority of the scrubbed
fluorine is retained by water droplets in the scrubbing systems and these

droplets may either be ejected from the top of the stack (thus still
polluting the environment) or drop back into the effluent through the
stack drain system.

All the scrubbers in the complex are being fitted with an abatement device
known as a "lute and swirler". This is essentially a spinning device which
captures droplets from the stack and spins them out, in a cyclone like
manner, for discharge into the liquid effluent. The device is likely to
reduce droplet emission (where the majority of the fluorine is contained)
by 90% or more and the anticipated cost of £4,500 per stack. Of course,
fluorine emissions in the liquid effluent may be expected to increase as
a consequence but to remain within permitted levels.

Environmental Considerations in the Dry Processes

Firm 1 - The compound fertilizer granulation plant

This granulation plant has an approximate capacity of 220 tonnes per day
and is capable of producing a complete range of compound formulations of
medium plant food concentration. It is a major potential source of dust
emissions to the atmosphere and extensive dust extraction hoods and
ducting are fitted to all possible sources of dust emission. Gases are
exhausted to a 36m stack at the rate of 220,000m^3/hr; these emissions are
substantially neutral, the white plume being mainly condensed steam from
the drying process. However, it should be noted that these are cleaned
emissions and arise after two stages of cleaning. First, the gases (with
a raw residual load of 250-500 kg/hr) of fertilizer dust pass through
cyclones with a design efficiency of 98-99% for the capture of dust and
particles exceeding 20 microns in diameter. However, these cyclones
require attention to bring operating efficiency up to the design level and
a figure of 90-92% efficiency would be nearer that achieved in practice.
The gases subsequently pass through a Doyle wet gas cleaning plant which
cleans the gases to a virtual zero content. This is a liquid recycling
scrubber and approximately 2m^3/hr of liquid effluent are discharged; this
effluent contains, for example, 300 ppm each of NH_4 and P_2O_5, depending
on the formulation of the compound being made. This represents
approximately 2 per cent of the total plant discharges.

Firm 4

This firm is part of a group of small fertilizer manufacturing companies
and is a typical small fertilizer manufacturer with a dry mixing process
producing 25,000 tonnes per year. Eight mixes of granular compound
fertilizer are produced but the type and N:P:K ratio depend on the inputs
which are ammonium sulphate, urea, M.A.P. superphosphate and muriate of
potash (potassium chloride). The products are usually coated with a thin
layer of clay.

The main pollutants from this plant are fertilizer and clay coating dust
and a liquid effluent containing small quantities of the various fertilizer
inputs. Dust problems arise at most of the individual units in the plant
(e.g. conditioner, dryer, cooler and coater) and from handling and packing.
A scrubber, which is intended to remove the sulphates, chlorides and
solids from the exhaust air, discharges waste water from its settlement
tank to the sea. Hot air is drawn through the dryer and exhausted directly

into the scrubber unit. In addition to this scrubber are six cyclones for dust collection. Most of the dust that arises is said to occur mainly from handling operations but the firm was unable to supply data on evolution rates. Much of the residue from the cyclones is recycled but some (especially the clay from the coatings) is not reusable and has to be dumped in a local tipping site.

The scrubber operated at about 98% efficiency. The dryer duct first draws off fumes and dust from the plant and heavy particles are cleaned by the cyclones. Gases and fumes pass through these and into the scrubber system, the core of which is a porous polystyrene/plastic section. Water flows down through this from sprays located just above it and scrubs out the gases filtering up. Gases not removed pass on up a 40m high tower for final discharge. A liquid effluent flows out of the bottom of the tower into a settlement tank from which it is recirculated at a rate of 180 l/min. The pH of this effluent is 5.5 and lime is added to neutralise it; waste water is discharged at sea. The settlement tank is cleaned out twice a year and the fertilizer sludge is taken by a local farmer.

Prior to the installation of the scrubber an old wash tower which consisted of three concrete towers containing water sprays was employed to reduce gaseous emissions. The installation of the scrubber has reduced gaseous emissions but a negative effect is a lower air velocity which in turn reduces the dispersion of what emissions there are.

Clearly there are two areas of cross-media transfer of pollution in this plant. First, the cyclones remove dust from exhaust air and this may be described as an air to solid transfer. However, the extent to which a trade-off arises is problematical since some of the captured material is reusable and it is quite possible that the firm would wish to reclaim some of these dusts, even in the absence of air pollution constraints. Second, the scrubber represents an air to water transfer and, because it is solely for pollution control purposes, almost certainly represents an environmental trade-off.

CHAPTER 4

Iron and Steel and Iron Founding

INTRODUCTION

A large number of water-borne residuals emanate from various stages of iron
and steel manufacture. Thus, in coking plants there are considerable
discharges of phenols, cyanides, thiocyanates, sulphides, oil and ammonia.
However, in most coking plants, water-borne residuals arise as a result of
the production process rather than of pollution control. Consequently,
there may have been cross-media transfers, but not cross-media trade-offs.
Similarly, in raw iron manufacturing there are substantial emissions of
particulates, ammonia, phenols, cyanides, sulphides and fluorides. However,
these are cleaned from the gas as a normal part of the raw iron
manufacturing process, since the blast furnace gas can be used if it is
cleaned adequately. Normally this cleaning occurs in a dry dust catcher
followed by a wet gas scrubber. In blast furnace operations air-borne
residuals are generated in the basic oxygen furnace and electric arc
furnace.

THE BASIC OXYGEN FURNACE

The air-borne residuals generated in this process are heat, fluxes, slag
particles, carbon monoxide, carbon dioxide and sub-micron iron fume.
Residuals are emitted when hot iron is poured into the ladles or furnace,
when sampling and temperature measurements are made, when steel is poured
into steel holding ladles, and when oxygen is injected into the furnace.
Approximately three per cent of steel production is ejected as dust and
fume, 85 per cent of which is fume of less than one micron. Electrostatic
precipitators and high-energy wet scrubbers are the two forms of control
device most used, although fabric filters may be used at transfer
operations where they have a high collection efficiency and a low energy
requirement. Precipitators also operate at relatively low energy inputs
and do not generate a steam plume; however, they need careful handling and
maintenance. Consequently, wet scrubbers may be used, which will require
an approximately 40 inch water column in order to achieve the required
reduction of emissions. This necessitates a large fan and, consequently,
the use of large amounts of energy. It generates a steam plume, which may

have a negative aesthetic impact on the environment and also produces a
slurry or iron oxide and water which has to be treated prior to discharge.
Solid wastes that are collected have to be dumped on a suitable tipping
site. Thus, in this instance, we have at least two cross-media transfers
caused by the operation of pollution control devices. In Table 4.1
we summarise some data collected from various sources, which will give an
indication of the quantities and parameters involved in a 'typical' plant.

THE ELECTRIC ARC FURNACE

High pressure is generated in the furnace when a charge is being heated,
melted and refined. This causes the emission of fine particulates through
openings round the electrode doors, etc. Emissions also take place when
the furnace is opened for charging or tilted for tapping. The amounts and
types of emissions generated depend on the melting rate, furnace temperature, the physical state of the fluxing agent and the extent to which
oxygen lancing is used. The greatest rate of emissions occurs during
oxygen lancing and melting. The raw loads of particulates varies from
three to eight kg/ton of steel without oxygen lancing and from five to
twenty kg/ton of steel with oxygen lancing. The fume is very fine with
95 per cent of particles less than half a micron. Around 60 per cent of
the dust consists of iron oxides and around 10 per cent is magnesium oxide.

There are clear cross-media trade-offs for alternative technologies: air
to water (in the case of wet scrubbers), air to air (in those cases
necessitating high levels of electric power), water to air (where electric
power is needed for liquid treatment). As already noted other factors
have also to be taken into account. Sometimes wet scrubbers result in an
aesthetically displeasing water-vapour plume. In some locations, liquid
wastes are easily and cheaply discharged out to sea with a high dispersion,
which probably results in low environmental cost and low cost of treatment.
Some of the technology types quoted are prone to breakdown or need heavy
maintenance. The electrostatic precipitators and bag filters on primary
air are examples of these. The power inputs for plants are based on data
supplied by the British Steel Corporation and are likely to reflect current
technology in use in the U.K. However, Environmental Protection Agency
sources suggest considerably lower energy requirements with some U.S.
plants and considerable research has reduced these inputs so much further
that energy inputs with new technology may possibly be 50 per cent of
those quoted.

Finally, it must be noted that several different types of equipment combine
to achieve a given level of efficiency. In particular, direct furnace
control and building evacuation are included together in our estimates,
although their marginal effectiveness and marginal energy inputs are
markedly different. Thus, building evacuation may increase emission
control efficiency by only a few percentage points but may have a cost
and power input several times higher than that of the primary control
equipment. In Table 4.2 the parameters of a typical plant are given.

IRON FOUNDING

The iron founding industry operates on a much smaller scale than the iron
and steel industry. The majority of cupolas are less than 7 tons per hour
capacity although over half of U.K. production is produced by cupolas of
larger size than this.

TABLE 4.1 Basic Oxygen Furnace

Process or control type	Residual load		Total control efficiency (%)	Cost (1972 $/t)	Energy inputs (Kwh/t)
Basic oxygen furnace (output 2.5 mt/y) (300 t/hour)	Particulates 31 kg/t		N/A	N/A	N/A
OPTION 1					
Venturi scrubber plus hooding and bag filters for building evacuation	Air (particulates) .15 kg/t		99.5%	3.35%	86
	Water	SS 9.6 kg/t Fl 0.9 kg/t pH 6-9			
	Solid	21.9 kg/t			
Liquid treatment using clarifier, once through polymer addition and lime precipitation	Air				
	Water	SS 0.1 kg/t Fl .01 kg/t¼ pH 6-9	99.9% on liquid	0.28%	1.4
	Solid	31.35 kg/t	100 % on solids	0.60	
Tipping	Air Water Solid Thermal	No change		.04	
OPTION 2					
Electrostatic precipitator and hooding and building evacuation	Air (particulates) .15 kg/t		99.5%	3.8	56.8
	Water	SS 0.5 Fl .04			
	Solid	31.1 kg/t			
Liquid treatment as in Option 1	Air Water Solid	No change Complete recycle 31.35 kg/t	100%	0.12	1.0
Tipping solid	Air Water Solid Thermal	No change	100%	0.60	.04

Source: OECD and British Steel Corporation

TABLE 4.2   Electric Arc Furnace

Process or control type	Residual load		Total control efficiency %	Cost kg/t (1972 $)	Energy inputs (Kwh/t)
Electric arc furnace (output 0.6 mt/year) (75 t/hour)	Total load 10 kg/t 1.23 kg/t particulates 6 kg/t iron oxide 1 kg/t magnesium oxide 1 kg/t zinc oxide 0.25 kg/t lead oxide 0.02 kg/t copper oxide 0.5 kg/t SO$_2$		N/A	N/A	N/A
OPTION 1 Baghouse primary and secondary	Air	0.1 kg/t	99.5	29.5	45.7
	Solid	9.9 kg/t			
Liquid			-		-
Solid tipping		-	100	0.56	-
Thermal		-	-	-	-
OPTION 2 Venturi plus building evacuation	Airborne	0.1 kg/t	99.5	8.90	86
	Water	SS 3.5 kg/t Fl 0.02 kg/t Zinc 0.02 kg/t pH 6-9			
	Solid	6.4 (settled out)			
Water treatment	Water	SS 0.1 kg/t pH 6-9	99.6	37/t	2.5
Tipping	Solid	9.9 kg/t	100	56	-
	Thermal	-	-	15	-

In essence the cupola is extremely simple and consists of a vertical
steel shaft usually refractory lined. Air is blown into the bottom of the
shaft through tuyeres while coke and iron in various forms and
proportions, with limestone as a fluxing agent, are charged into the top
of the shaft. The coke is burned by the tuyere air and melts the charge
materials which descend the shaft by gravity and are replaced by fresh
charges. The molten metal runs out of a tap hole at the very bottom of the
shaft below the tuyeres.

The cupola not only melts the metal charged into it but also alters its
composition. Elements such as carbon and sulphur are absorbed in varying
degrees by the metal, whilst others, notably silicon, are partially removed
by oxidation. The melting of iron of the right composition and temperature
requires very careful control of charge materials and melting conditions.
The solid particulate matter emitted with the combustion gases varies
with the charge materials and operation of the furnaces. It is not,
therefore, possible to predict with accuracy the amount and composition of
the particles as they will vary from cupola to cupola and with time.

The main emissions from cupolas are:-

(i)   Grit: Particles of over 75 microns in size are defined as grit.
Half or more by weight of the solids emitted by cupolas are in this range
and are easily collected by simple means. Grit is made up predominantly
of coke particles; sand, limestone, rust and small debris which may
accumulate in the stock yard and may eventually be charged into the cupola
along with other materials.

(ii)   Dust: Dust is defined as being larger than one micron in size and
therefore particles above one micron and below 75 microns are said to be
dust. Cupola dust is made up largely of the same substances as cupola
grit but usually contains more of the trace elements to be found in
cupola charge materials, e.g. non-ferrous metals. Being smaller, the dust
fraction is more difficult to collect than grit but a high proportion by
weight can be collected by medium efficiency fan-powered systems such as
multi-cyclones or medium intensity scrubbers.

(iii)   Metallurgical fume: Fume is generated in the cupola melting zone
and is quite different in appearance from the generally angular grit and
dust. It is physically similar to the oxide fume generated in the oxygen
steelmaking processes but consists of other materials as well as iron
oxide. In particular, many metallic oxides and silicates can be identified.
The amount of fume generated by cupolas varies and appears to depend
primarily on the proportions of coke and steel charged and on contaminants
such as zinc in the metallic charge. As an approximation, a typical
cupola using 15 per cent coke (as a percentage of the weight of metal
charged) and 20 per cent steel is likely to emit 1 kg of metallurgical
fume for every tonne melted.

(iv)   Smoke: Only in a few cases is it economically possible to use
completely clean materials. Much of the iron and steel scrap available to
the foundry industry is contaminated and since no economical method of
removing carbonaceous materials is used, outputs of smoke are emitted.

Control devices

There are a variety of both dry and wet systems available for use in this
industry. The Grit and Dust Working Party established that cupolas of
different sizes should have to fit control devices of varying efficiency
levels. Thus they found it acceptable that a small 3 ton per hour cupola
should use a simple wet arrester whereas a 20 ton per hour cupola had to
use the high efficiency venturi scrubber. Medium sized cupolas could use
a variety of dry systems such as multi-cyclones; electrostatic precipitators
and bag filters could of course be used but in fact the industry has not
accepted these on any scale because of the economic and technical problems
involved.

We collected data on iron founding pollution control from several sources
but only include one composite case covering all of these. In this
composite case we have initially set out data in a form that can be used
later on in the 'Delphi' study although in the second part of the case
some individual aspects of control as they have related to specific plant
choices have been detailed. The technological alternatives discussed are
to a certain extent determined by the size of plant. This is because
the recommendations of the Grit and Dust working party suggested different
levels of emission control efficiency for different sized cupolas.
Thus a twenty tonne per hour cupola would not (by 1982) be allowed to be
fitted only with a simple wet arrester nor would it be necessary to fit a
three tonne per hour cupola with a venturi scrubber. However comparisons
of the cross-media effects of control equipment can still be made by
taking multiples of different plant sizes.

IRON FOUNDING: COMPOSITE CASE

Part (a) Economic and Technological Parameters

Four cupolas of different melting rates have been postulated in this
composite case using a likely (but not exclusive) type of gas cleaning
plant for the size and type of cupola.

1   A 3 tonne/hour cold-blast cupola fitted with a simple wet
       arrester, of collection efficiency 55 per cent. The cupola has
       been assumed to operate for five hours per day, i.e. to melt
       75 tonnes of metal per week. The gases leaving the stack in
       the shaft are diluted by 200 per cent and burnt to remove
       carbon monoxide.

2   A 7 tonne/hour cold-blast cupola fitted with a dry multicyclone
       gas cleaning plant of collection efficiency 85 per cent. This
       cupola is assumed to operate for 8 hours per day, a weekly total
       of 280 tonnes of metal. In the gas cleaning plant the offtake
       gases are taken off above the cupola charge door and cooled
       by air dilution to less than 320°C. The dilution is 800 per cent
       and carbon monoxide is burnt.

3   A 15 tonne/hour cold-blast cupola fitted with either a high
       efficiency wet venturi scrubber (collection efficiency 98.5
       per cent), in which the gases are cooled by water saturation,
       or a fabric filter (collection efficiency 99.9 per cent) in
       which the gases are cooled in a heat exchanger. The gases from
       this cupola are taken off above the charge, with a dilution

of 250 per cent and combustion taking place. Melting is for
8 hours daily, to give a weekly tonnage of 600 tonnes.

4   A 20 tonne/hour hot-blast cupola fitted with a scrubber
        equivalent to a high pressure venturi, such as a Theissen
        Disintegrator (collection efficiency 98.5 per cent) or a fabric
        filter (collection efficiency 99.9 per cent). Gases entering
        the scrubber are cooled by water saturation, and entering the
        fabric filter are cooled by heat exchanger. This cupola melts
        for 8 hours per day, to produce 800 tonnes of metal per week.
        Below charge offtakes are used, giving a gas dilution of
        10 per cent with no combustion. Fabric filters have rarely
        been used in the foundry industry in the U.K. because of the
        necessity of cooling the gases, and the distinct possibility
        of bag filter fires occurring.

All four cupolas have been assumed to operate at a coke/metal ratio of
12 per cent, and the respective blast rates are therefore 2 400m^3/hr,
5 500m^3/hr, 12 000m^3/hr and 14 500m^3/hr.

Other assumptions made include an uncontrolled emission of 8kg of
particulates/tonne of iron melted. The hot-blast cupola is not
recuperative, i.e. the blast is independently heated.

Table 4.3 shows the basic information of the four cupolas. The gas flows
and temperature shown in Table 4.3a have been calculated and include
dilution air, combustion and saturation with water vapour where appropriate.
The quantities of SO_2 in the offtake gases have been calculated using the
estimates in the publication "Cold-blast Cupolas" (Ministry of Housing and
Local Government, HMSO 1968; now out of print), and assuming that a simple
wet arrester removes 50 per cent of SO_2 and high efficiency wet scrubbers
remove 95 per cent of SO_2. From these two tables we have derived Tables
4.3b and 4.3c which contain cost effectiveness data.

IRON FOUNDING: SPECIFIC CASE

This case has been almost entirely data based and consequently little
comment has been possible on the damage to the environment the alternative
discharges generate. However, it is clear that there are various wet and
dry alternatives which have differing cross-media impacts. In particular
the choice between the venturi operating on the fifteen tonne per hour
cupola can be compared to the multi-cyclone on the seven tonne per hour,
whilst a more direct cross-media comparison can be made on the twenty
tonne per hour hot blast cupola between the high pressure venturi and the
bag filter plant.

Not all the relevant environmental input-output parameters have been
discussed previously, because of the composite nature of the data. Thus
the noise from the control equipment, the chimney height, the method and
place of the liquid and solids discharge are all factors which are likely
to affect an environmental evaluation of the alternative technologies.
In this industry there is considerable heterogeneity of location because
of the historic roots which affected the nature of the industry's growth;
consequently local factors may be very important as they affect environmental impact.

TABLE 4.3   Basic Information Concerning the Four Cupola Plants

Cupola Melting Rate t/h	3	7	15	20
Hours melted/week	25	40	40	40
Tonnes melted/week	75	280	600	800
Coke Rate %	12	12	12	12
Blast Rate m³/h at S.T.P.	2400	5500	12000	14500
Uncontrolled emission rate kg/t	8	8	8	8
Temperature of gases entering gas cleaning plant °C	800	320, say 250	800 venturi 240 fabric filter	300 Disintegrator 240 Fabric filter
Slag produced, kg/t	62.5	62.5	62.5	62.5

Source: B.C.I.R.A. and Department of Industry

TABLE 4.3a Details of Gas Flows and Temperature etc.

Cupola	3 t/h with simple wet arrester	7 t/h with multicyclone plant	15 t/h with (a) Venturi Scrubber (b) Fabric Filter	20 t/h with (a) Venturi scrubber (b) Fabric Filter
Gas flow before air dilution and combustion m^3/h	2,500	5,700	12,300	15,900
Gas flow after dilution and combustion, corrected to 15°C m^3/h	6,900	48,000	27,000	16,500 (no combustion)
Saturated exhaust gas flow rate corrected to 15°C m^3/h	7,600	48,000	(a) 45,600 Venturi scrubber (b) 27,000 Fabric filter	(a) 18,200 Disintegrator (b) 16,500 Fabric filter
Exhaust gas temperature °C	300	250 (maximum 320)	(a) 77 Venturi (b) 240 Fabric filter	(a) 25 Disintegrator (b) 240 Fabric filter
SO_2 in offtake gas kg/h	0.06	0.3	(a) 0.6 (b) 0.6	(a) 0.8 (b) 0.8
SO_2 emitted to atmosphere kg/h	0.03	0.3	(a) 0.6 (b) 0.03	(a) 0.8 (b) 0.04

Source: B.C.I.R.A. and Department of Industry

TABLE 4.3b Collection of Particulates etc. by Gas Cleaning Plant

	3 t/h with simple wet arrester	7 t/h with multicyclone plant	15 t/h with (a) Venturi Scrubber (b) Fabric Filter	20 t/h with (a) Venturi Scrubber (b) Fabric Filter
Assumed collection efficiency %	55	85	(a) 98.5 (b) 99.9	(a) 98.5 (b) 99.9
Emission to atmosphere kg/t	3.7	1.1	(a) 0.12 (b) 0.01	(a) 0.12 (b) 0.01
kg/h	11	8	(a) 1.8 (b) 0.12	(a) 2.4 (b) 0.16
Concentration of solids in cleaned gas mg/Nm^3	1450	170	(a) 40 (b) 5	(a) 130 (b) 10
Wt of solids collected kg/t dry / kg/week	— / —	6.9 / 1930	(b) 7.99 (b) 4800	(b) 7.99 (b) 6400
Wt of solids collected kg/t wet / kg/week	4.3 / 320	— / —	(a) 7.9 (a) 4740	(a) 7.9 (a) 6320
Wt of solids tipped on a dry basis kg/t / kg/week	3.9 / 290	6.9 / 1930	(a) 7.1 (b) 7.99 (a) 4260 (b) 4740	(a) 7.1 (b) 7.99 (a) 5680 (b) 6320
Wt of slag produced (to tip) weekly (tonnes)	4.7	17.5	37.5	50.0
Energy input of cleaning plant (kw/h)	3 (1 kwh/t)	38 (5.4 kwh/t)	(a) 240 (16 kwh/t) (b) 180 (12 kwh/t)	(a) 300 (15 kwh/t) (b) 225 (11.3 kwh/t)

Source: B.C.I.R.A. and Department of Industry

TABLE 4.3c Details of Water Usage in Gas Cleaning Plants

		3 t/h with simple wet arrester	7 t/h with multicyclone plant	15 t/h with (a) Venturi Scrubber Fabric Filter (b) Fabric Filter	20 t/h with (a) Venturi Scrubber (b) Fabric Filter
Water tank capacity	kg	9,000	—	23,000	23,000
Evaporation losses	kg/t	270	—	(a) 890	(a) 390
	kg/week	20,000	—	(a) 534,000	(a) 312,000
Frequency of draining tank		weekly	—	weekly	weekly
Total water usage	kg/t	390	—	930	420
	kg/week	29,250	—	557,000	335,000
Wt of water tipped weekly	kg	9,000	—	23,000	23,000
% solids in tipped water, maximum		0.4	—	2.1	2.8
Costs Capital		20,000	100,000	210,000	260,000
Running costs (1 shift per day)	£	3,500	25,000	60,000	78,000
Annualised Cost	£	6,800	41,700	95,000	121,000
Cost per ton	£	1.81	2.98	3.17	3.03

Source: B.C.I.R.A. and Department of Industry

One firm we visited which was operating a three tonne per hour cupola was situated in a pleasant rural valley close to residential housing. The firm employed 70 workers and provided local employment. Some years ago the firm installed a simple wet arrestor which prevented emission of smoke via a stack 65 feet high. In terms of total efficiency, this operated at probably less than 60 per cent. Because of the location of the plant the fumes were still emitted at a height which could cause problems for nearby householders. The wet arrester yielded almost 6,000 gallons of waste water per week (2 loads per week) which, until recently, had been tankered and sent to a tip about 10 miles away.

The local authority controlling the tip had withdrawn permission for the firm to dump this large amount of liquid on the tip because of possible leaching problems. The constituents of the waste water are shown in Table 4.4.

TABLE 4.4 Actual Waste Water Characteristics

	mg/l
Cadmium	0.11
Chlorine	0.14
Copper	1.46
Nickel	0.21
Zinc	17.00
Lead	13.7
Barium	1.20
COD	200
SS	1,114.00
pH	7.6

The water authorities would not allow this to be tipped directly to sewer unless it fell within the following parameters.

TABLE 4.5 Waste Water Parameters Required for Discharge to Sewer

Vol.	5.00m³ per day		
	0.3m³ per day		
Total metals excluding zinc 6.0 mg/l			
Cadmium 1.0	Chrome 5.0		Copper 2.0
Ni 0.5	Zn 3.0		
400 mg/Sulphate			pH range 6 - 9

The firm would have had to install its own waste treatment plant to achieve the above parameters for its effluent, so instead they developed a simple settlement system with a drag out conveyor which allowed most of the solid residuals to be separated from the liquid. Much of the liquid was then allowed to evaporate away and water changes only had to be made every three months. The solid residuals, which were almost in a dry state, were then taken to a tip for dumping. As this could be included in the day to

day tipping of foundry slag the marginal cost of this extra amount was very
small. Indeed the whole operation resulted in a situation where the firm
was saving £1,752* per year in tankering charges and was incurring an
annualised cost of approximately £222 for its settlement conveyor drag out
(which had a total cost of £5,219 and would last approximately 10 years).

This firm had also considered alternative dry systems (including changing to
an electric furnace) but all were too expensive. This specific case
provides an interesting example of cross-media trade-offs proving
unacceptable but where the firm concerned was able to overcome the problem
by a technological change which eventually led to net cost savings. It
also illustrates how cross-media trade-offs can be important to relatively
small companies, as well as the very large ones.

In another firm we visited choice of control equipment type which affected
the distribution of cross-media transfers had been exercised at two stages.
This was a relatively large firm which some time ago had elected to invest
in electric melting partly because of the lower pollution levels generated.
Environmental pollution was a particular cause for concern in this
case because the firm was situated close to residential housing development. The electric melters, whilst not emitting large quantities of
grit and dust like the cold blast cupolas still gave off substantial
emissions of fine iron oxide fume and in addition required 3 megawatts
per hour (750 Kw per one tonne per hour melted) of electic power (which of
course will lead to sulphur oxide and fly ash pollution at and around coal
fired power stations. Workplace conditions also seemed adversely affected
by this particular technology choice in this case.

In addition capital costs are between three and four times higher for
electric melting. Figures quoted to us by firms suggested that for ten
tonne per hour melting a cold blast cupola would have a capital cost of
£250,000 whilst an electric furnace would cost almost £800,000. Running
costs for the latter would be approximately 5 per cent higher. However, if
a high pressure venturi scrubber was fitted to the cold blast cupola the
total cost would be over £550,000. The environmental and economic impact
of electric melting in the foundry industry is an issue that is outside the
scope of this book, however it is clear that electric melting can
sometimes be more expensive and lead to pollution of a different type and
distribution to that coming from a cold blast cupola. Consequently there
are intra media trade-offs which occur because of this type of technology
choice which involves an assessment of the impact of finer fume with a less
widespread (and therefore more concentrated) distribution and high
associated electricity costs, as opposed to more visible particulate and
fume which may be distributed over a wider area.

In this same instance the firm had also to choose an arrestment device for
its ten tonne per hour cold blast cupola. The basic choice lay between
three alternatives: (a) A high efficiency wet scrubber which would achieve
9& per cent efficiency on fine as well as coarse fume (down to 3 microns).
The cost of this including installation was £350,000, excluding treatment
facilities for the resulting liquid waste. (b) A bag filter system with
a slightly lower capital and operating cost but which because of its
inapplicability to foundry emissions (which could cause baghouse fires

---

* All cost data in this case are quoted in 1978 prices.

and holes in the bags) was rejected at an early stage. (c) A medium
efficiency dry system which operated at 98 per cent efficiency on 10 micron
fume but was much less efficient on the finer fume as Table 4.6 below
illustrates.

TABLE 4.6   Canadian Cool Cap Arrestment Efficiency

10 tonnes per hour melting

grit and dust (lbs per hour) (10 microns +)	5.6 - 6.4
fume emission	17.6 - 18.1
concentration of emissions	0.108 grains/foot^3

The capital cost of this system was only £120,000, with minimum maintenance
costs, and power costs less than (a). In addition it would not generate
any liquid waste and produced only 8 cubic yards of dry dust for dumping
per week. Emissions were not quite invisible but they were colourless and
in the various instances we encountered this control device being used
emissions did not provide a basis for complaints from local residents.

The firm in this instance chose and installed the dry system. Clearly on
pure commercial grounds this was the best choice but it was also interesting
to note that the local environmental health officer encouraged this choice
because of the potential damage secondary wet residuals might cause if
disposed of in this particular locality whilst the water authority were
reluctant to accept any·discharges of this to the sewers. It seems that
to a certain extent damage to various environmental media had been compared
and the higher efficiency (and higher cost) of the wet system on fume of
less than 10 microns was not considered adequate justification for
installing a high pressure venturi scrubber if it resulted in a secondary
liquid disposal problem.

CONCLUSIONS

We have been able to identify several sources of cross-media trade-offs as
they emanate from environmental control in the iron, steel and iron
founding industries. In the main the trade-offs occur through the use
of wet scrubbers on airborne emissions although there are considerable
intra media trade-offs as higher levels of pollution control efficiency
require greater and greater inputs of electricity; the production of which
is itself pollution intensive. Both the inter and intra forms of cross-
media transfer are especially important in this industry because frequently
a relatively inert but aesthetically displeasing airborne emission is
controlled at high pecuniary cost and can also generate substantial
pollution when it is concentrated in water courses following wet scrubbing
and/or tipping of sludges.

Over the last decade substantial advances have been made with ·electric
melting which provides less primary pollution than traditional methods in
this industry. However it does have implications for secondary pollutants
emanating from power stations and consequently this too can be seen as an
in-plant control device which has some cross-media implications.

The size and distribution of plants in these two industries means that most areas are subject to small amounts of pollution from the production of iron, steel, or iron castings. However the major concentrations of pollution only occur at a few places where large complexes have been established and it is in these locations that the industry is still a major polluter of the environment.

CHAPTER 5

Energy Requirements of Pollution Control Equipment

INTRODUCTION

An increasing source of pollution trade-offs are those that arise from the use of electricity to achieve higher levels of collection efficiency in both air, water and solid pollution control. These may be either inter or intra media trade-offs due to the emissions of sulphur oxides, fly ash, and nitrogen oxides from conventional power generation. Their magnitude and importance must necessarily depend on the method of electricity generation and the pollution control devices operative at power stations. These are difficult to generalise on and within the scope of this book only a preliminary investigation is possible. For instance it is the pollution output of the marginal power station that is the relevant trade-off factor, but within the confines of our national grid this will change with the time of day, season etc. We can, however, be reasonably certain that most marginal power stations are coal fired and that these will use electrostatic precipitators for fly ash removal and high dispersal for sulphur and nitrogen oxides. The other major factor of importance in any environmental cost benefit analysis is that concerned with resource conservation and energy saving. This must also remain outside the scope of this chapter although it has been the focus of several studies in the last few years. Here we merely attempt to evaluate the relationship between the energy requirements for marginal levels of pollution removal in specific industries and the consequent marginal output of pollutants from the power generation. These relationships are clearly important and some attempt at estimating some of the damage created by secondary pollution generation is given in the next chapter when an evaluation is made of the human health effects of sulphur oxides and smoke.

ENVIRONMENTAL ENERGY REQUIREMENTS

The EPA classifies the energy requirements of pollution control into three categories. These are Direct In Plant, Indirect In Plant and Indirect Post Plant. The two latter (indirect categories) relate in the case of Indirect Post Plant to the energy requirements needed to dispose of the solid/liquid waste that arise from the operation of a pollution control device. We can

TABLE 5.1 Air Pollution Equipment Power Requirements

	Pollutants Treated	Power Required * kW/1,000 scfm Typical range
Exhaust stacks	Dispersion of particulates and gases	0
Baghouses, cloth filters etc.	Fume	0.1 - 1.0
Electrostatic precipitators		
High voltage	Particulates and	0.2 - 0.6
Low voltage	Fume	0.01 - 0.04
Scrubbers	Particulates, vapours, mists gases, fumes	1 to 12
Adsorption beds	Hydrocarbons, fumes, gases, vapours	100 to 200 Btu/lb adsorbent to heat to 600°F without heat exchange
Fume afterburners	Fumes and mists gases, fumes, organic vapours	2 to 5 3 to 8×10^5 Btu/hr 1.0 to 1.4×10^6 Btu/hr
Catalytic oxidizers	Gases, fumes, organic vapours	1.3×10^5 Btu/hr 0 to 1.0×10^6 Btu/hr
Condensers and cold traps	Vapours, gases	None

Source: F.I. Honea, Energy Requirements for Environmental Control
         Equipment, Chemical Engineering Deskbook, October, 1974

*In addition to the usual energy requirements there will also be a fan
power requirement for pressure drop encountered. We have not included
these in this table for ease of exposition.

TABLE 5.2   Wastewater-treatment Equipment

Equipment	Power
Wastewater systems	
Closed system	10 to 25 kW/1,000 gal
Open system—settling pond	5 to 10 kW/1,000 gal
Agitators	Mild: 0.37 to 0.75 kW/1,000 gal
	Vigorous: 1.5 to 2.2 kW/1,000 gal
	Intense: 3 to 7.5 kW/1,000 gal
	Normal: 2.0 kW/1,000 gal
Aerators	
General lagoon	0.5 to 20 kW/million gal
Surface aerator	4 to 5.5 lb oxygen/kWh
Submerged turbine	
single impeller	2 to 2.7 lb/kWh
dual impeller	3.3 to 4 lb/kWh
Screens	
Stationary	None
Shaking, vibrating	0.04 to 0.10 kW/ft^2
Filters	
Trickling, sand bed	None, unless to drive spray arm
Continuous, vacuum, belt or drum	Rotation: 0.04 kW/ft^2
Intermittent:	
press	None
clarifying, incline	None
Thickeners and clarifiers	
Gravity thickener, lagoons	None
Thickener	0.4 to 12 kW/1,000 gpm
Clarifier	0.4 to 12 kW/1,000 gpm
Separators	
Centrifugal	0.2 to 25 kWh/ton solids
Adsorption	Regeneration:
Zeolites, carbon	100 to 200 Btu/h
Activated charcole	per lb dry adsorbent
Distillation	50 to 1,200 Btu/lb
Reverse osmosis	None
Chemical treatment	Metering pumps, agitation (mixing)

Source: F.I. Honea, op.cit

only make very tentative estimates of these two categories, although
evidence suggests they can be substantial, consequently we concentrate
on the Direct In Plant which is the category which covers the energy
requirements of pollution control equipment (either in plant or end of line)
when it is in use.   There are a very large number of types of pollution
control equipment and an indication of these and the nature of their energy
requirements is given in Tables 5.1 and 5.2 below.   This data generally
relates to plant and equipment used in the U.S.A., comparable general
data for the U.K. is given in Table 5.3 and is based on some pioneering
work in this area by Stairmand and other authors who used his data.
This data is now dated, however we present it since its coverage is
excellent and the relative magnitudes are likely to be useful indicators.

It would be useful to develop a functional relationship between energy
inputs and pollution removal; however it must be remembered that this
cannot be really seen in terms of a continuous function since in the
vast majority of cases the type of equipment as well as the electricity
input has to be changed.   Thus at best we can only develop a quasi
discrete function; each item of control equipment having a small range
of control efficiency, with substantial changes only being possible by a
change to a different type of control.   Only with venturi scrubbers can
we really attempt to match marginal electricity inputs with a continuous
and increasing degree of control, and even this is only over a limited
range.   Finally it must be remembered that different types of pollution
control equipment operate with varying cost/effectiveness depending on
the particle size of fume; consequently where possible efficiencies for
different sizes is given.

TABLE 5.3   Pollution Control, Efficiency and Direct
Electricity Inputs at Various Particle Sizes

	Efficiency on standard dust (microns)			Electricity Input
	50	5	1	(kwh)/hr
Inertial collector	95	16	3	19.5
High efficiency cyclone	96	73	27	56.5
Jet impingement scrubber	98	83	40	93.8
Self induced spray deduster	100	94	48	70.5
Spray tower	99	94	55	59.5
Fluidised bed scrubber	99	98	58	38.8
Irrigated target scrubber	100	97	80	72.5
Electrostatic collector	99	99	86	25.0
Disintegrator	100	98	91	567.5
Flooded disc scrubber - low energy	100	99	96	146.8
Venturi scrubber - medium energy	100	99	97	235.3
Flooded disc scrubber - medium energy	100	99	97	241.8
Venturi scrubber - high energy	100	99	98	371.8

Source: C J Stairmand, The Chemical Engineer, December 1965

Whilst there are exceptions (for instance the high energy venturi scrubber
and the bag filter) overall increased collection efficiency can be seen
from the tables to be related to an exponentially increasing input of

electricity. From this functional form we can estimate at different levels of efficiency the electricity input elasticity of increased control. Policymakers could then translate this into a trade-off between the damage caused by the pollutants emanating from electricity generation and the damage prevented by using pollution control. Clearly no conclusions can be reached at this stage since in this section of this chapter we are only dealing with the problem at a general level. In the next section, however, when particular processes are specified, we then have the data with which specific comparisons can be made.

ENERGY REQUIREMENTS FOR POLLUTION CONTROL IN SPECIFIC INDUSTRIES

In this section we look specifically at the pollution implications of energy that is required to abate particular pollutants in a sample of industries where pollution abatement is relatively energy intensive. Consequently it is necessary to (a) develop estimates of the pollution output from power generation, (b) estimate marginal pollution control energy requirements in particular industries, (c) substitute the data developed in (a) and (b) in order to show what pollutants are produced when other pollutants are prevented. This is essentially an intra media trade-off that has largely been ignored by policy makers who have been concerned with solving one problem in the environment without paying attention to problems created in completely separate industries. A starting point must, therefore, be an evaluation of the pollution output created in generating electricity.

Below are estimates of the pollution output of a coal fired 1000 megawatt power station using an electrostatic precipitator and high dispersal. These data are probably higher than for an average U.K. power plant but may be a good indicator of the pollutant outputs of the less efficient.

TABLE 5.4 Pollutant Output From a Coal Fired Power Plant Using an Electrostatic Precipitator

Airborne Pollutants	Kg per Kilowatt hour
NO_x	.00314
SO_2	.0194
CO^2	.000176
Flyash	.000418
Total organic	.000055
Heat	1,196 Bthu/hour

Waterborne pollutants	
Suspended solids	nil
Dissolved solids	.00002
Total organics	.00001
Inorganics	.00005
Heat	4,600 Bthu/hour

Land	
Ash	.0497

Source: Battelle Columbus Laboratories

Primary aluminium

The primary aluminium industry is highly energy intensive, In a recent
U.S. survey it was ranked eighth in energy intensity in the U.S.A.
consuming 108 billion (10^9) kWh of electricity annually. (I) The
major pollutants from aluminium production are solid and gaseous fluorides.
Though these do not, in current concentrations, constitute a major hazard
to humans, they have caused severe problems to livestock, and fluoride
control has been a major area of environmental concern in the U.K. and
the U.S.A. In 1972, in the U.S.A., 1.14 billion kWh of electricity was
used to control air pollution from primary aluminium pots. This increased
in 1976 to 2.2 billion kWh following a tightening of controls. Proposed
new source performance standards will further increase this energy input
to 5.3 billion kWh.

Pollution control equipment for aluminium reduction can be divided into
primary and secondary systems. The primary system removes the majority
of the fume emitted directly from the pot, and the secondary system
collects the emissions which escape from primary systems. The emissions
which escape the primary hooding are of a low pollutant concentration,
the volume of air drafted through a pot-room building being about ten
times the amount of air drafted through the primary control system. A
secondary system thus has a much larger volume of air to treat, which is
also of a lower pollutant concentration. For these reasons, secondary
systems are energy intensive and inefficient compared to the primary
control scrubber.

TABLE 5.5   Direct U.S. Aggregate Energy Requirements for
            Air Pollution Control by Plant Type and Control
            Level (million kWh/year)

Plant Type	4.1 kg/ tonne	1.6 kg/ tonne	0.9 kg/ tonne
Centre-worked prebake	564	921	2,063
Side-worked prebake	161	291	364
Vertical spiked Soderberg	107	212	1,684
Horizontal spiked Soderberg	309	787	1,150
Total	1,140	2,211	5,260

Source: Energy Requirements for Air Pollution Control in Primary
          Aluminium, U.S. Department of Commerce, Washington,DC, 1977

The energy inefficiency of the secondary control system is readily apparent
when one compares its energy consumption per kg of pollutant removal with
that of a primary system. A broad estimate from U.S. data suggests that
the primary system might remove 97% of fluorine emissions, at an energy
usage of 200 kWh per tonne of aluminium. To achieve a further 1% increase
in efficiency would necessitate a secondary system with a mimimum
incremental electricity input of 100 kWh per tonne of aluminium. This
sort of system is one which can only yield quite small benefits to the
immediate environment that would have been impacted by fluoride emissions.
Table 5.5 illustrates for various production processes in the U.S.A. the
aggregate energy requirements for increasing degrees of pollution
control in primary aluminium.

Further control has been demonstrated to be possible to reduce fluoride
emissions even more (2). However, it is likely that the energy requirements for this would be out of proportion to the benefits achieved. For
a maximum output of I kg pollutant per tonne of aluminium produced, the
environmental risk of the fluoride emissions is probably minimal,
particularly if it is also subject to high dispersal.

A more specific energy analysis of various forms of air pollution control
used in the primary aluminium industry in Europe is given in Table 5.6.
While the actual inputs and outputs differ slightly from the previous data,
there is still considerable evidence of exponentially increasing energy
usage for pollution control systems when they achieve very high levels of
efficiency.

TABLE 5.6   Energy Usage by Different Pollution Control
              Technologies in Primary Aluminium

Type of equipment	Overall control efficiency (% total fluoride)	Energy use on prebake pots (kWh/tonne)	Total pollution control costs (1975 $/tonne)
Primary control system			
Multicyclone	32	34	8.98
Floating bed scrubber	73	40	8.35
Spray tower	85	24	4.24
Multicyclone and dry electrostatic precipitator	90	70	16.99
Venturi scrubber	90	345	18.76
Injected alumina scrubber	94	65	13.39
Fluidized bed scrubber	95	161	13.39
Primary and secondary control system			
Dry electrostatic precipitator spray screen and spray tower	94	222	36.02
Injected alumina dry scrubber and spray screen	96	250	37.16
Fluidized bed dry scrubber and spray screen	97	347	37.16

Source: The data result indirectly from Pollution Control Costs in
Primary Aluminium Industry, OECD, Paris, 1977

Tables 5.5 and 5.6 illustrate the sharply increasing energy usage
associated with pollution control (as well as increasing cost) as control
efficiencies of 90 per cent and above are reached. As an example, to
increase fluoride collection efficiency from 95% to 97% would necessitate
the addition of a spray screen to the fluidized bed scrubber. This
would result in a reduction of fluoride from about I kg/tonne of aluminium
produced to 0.6 kg/tonne - an environmental reduction of 0.4 kg fluoride/
tonne of aluminium. The impact on the environment of achieving this with
the energy intensive method suggested would be to increase emissions to
the environment (see Table 5.7).

TABLE 5.7   Secondary Pollutant Outputs Arising from an
Increase in Pollution Control in Primary Aluminium
Using Fluidized Bed Scrubber and Spray Screen

Airborne pollutants	Pollutants per tonne aluminium (kg)
NO_x	0.5
SO_2	3.61
CO^2	0.03
Fly ash	0.08
Total organics	0.01
Heat	22 456 (Btu)

Waterborne	
Suspended solids	Nil
Dissolved solids	0.003 72
Total organics	0.001 86
Inorganics	0.009 30
Heat	828 000 (Btu)

Land	
Ash	9.24

Note: These figures are obtained by multiplying the data in Table 5.4 by
the relevant marginal electricity usage required for pollution control
from Table 5.6.

Some of the pollutants emanating from increased energy output may be
subject to high dispersal or may be used in roadbuilding and construction.
However, it still seems likely that pollution output from increased energy
usage is greater than the pollution prevented by more efficient technologies. An application of the environmental weightings described in
earlier chapters would emphasise this.

Iron and Steel and Iron Founding

Like primary aluminium the iron and steel industry is a large energy user
and because increasing control standards have demanded building evacuation
its pollution control is highly electricity intensive. Chapter 4 has
already given an indication of the magnitudes involved, consequently we
refer the reader to this data but also introduce some new data that is
relevant.

The basic air pollution control devices and their electricity usage in
this industry are given in Table 5.8 below.

TABLE 5.8 Energy Usage per Unit of Air Treated

Control device*	Energy per unit of air treated (KwH/million SCF)
High-energy scrubber	239.2
Electrostatic precipitator	49.2
Fabric filter	46.4
Medium-energy scrubber	45.1

*A low-energy scrubber is used to control power plant SO_2. Although the device is called a low-energy scrubber, its energy per unit of air flow is 376.5 KwH/million SCF, which is significantly higher than the other devices. The energy consumed is used to operate blowers, pumps, exhaust gas rehead, and sludge removal equipment.

Source: Energy requirements for Environmental Control in the Iron and Steel Industry. U.S. Department of Commerce, 1976.

Additionally Table 5.9 relates to a small electric arc furnace using bag filters for building evacuation which as can be seen from the previous table, are not particularly intensive in electricity. The data shown in the table below relate to technology proposed by the U.S. Environmental Protection Agency to help reduce emissions from steel plants using electric arc furnaces. They refer to three systems, (a) a D.E.C. system which involves direct furnace evacuation connected to a bag house, (b) canopy hooding which is an adjunct to a bag house but which increases collection efficiency, and (c) a roof scavenger which would normally be attached to both (a) and (b). There are very substantial increasing costs of control and inputs of electricity. The trade-off at the higher level of control is between .0105 kg/te of a relatively inert fume on the one hand and .05 kg/te of NO_x, .3104 kg/te of SO_2 and .795 kg/te of slag as well as some lesser pollutants (details of which are in Table 5. 4)

Once again it seems unlikely that the higher level of control could possibly be a best environmental option. Indeed in view of the relatively harmless nature of the basic pollutant the optimum level of control is likely to be substantially less than that proposed in this instance.

TABLE 5.9   Energy Input and Costs of Control for a Small Electric Arc Furnace

	DEC System	Canopy Hoods		Building Evacuation	
	Total	Total	Marginal	Total	Marginal
Efficiency%	87.8	97.3	9.5	97.4	0.1
Kg of dust collected per tonne of steel	9.98	11.06	1.08	11.07	0.0105
Annual cost $/kg of dust	0.078	1.09	1.01	74.3	73.2
$/kg of steel	0.77	1.78	1.01	2.55	0.77
Electricity required KwH/kg of dust	.255	17.1	16.85	1517.2	1500.4
KwH/te of steel	2.552	20.79	18.24	36.47	15.68

Source: An adaptation from J E Barber, Zero Visible Emissions: Energy Requirements, Economics and Environmental Impact. Engineering Aspects of Pollution Control in the Metals Industry. Metals Society 1975

Other Industries

In various chapters of this book we have dealt with the iron founding and fertilizer industries. It is not intended to add much extra information to this data in this chapter. Where the data was available we have quoted electricity usage as it relates to pollution control. This is particularly interesting in the case of iron founding because the pollutant prevented is relatively innocuous and the controls used do not involve the very energy energy intensive options involved with building evacuation, although because of the nature of the fume Venturi Scrubbers may be used. It is clear from discussions in the initial parts of this chapter that Venturi Scrubbers are very energy intensive. Some recent evidence from the U.S.A. shows how in the context of an iron foundry increased levels of collection efficiency in excess of 95 per cent have several energy implications for the firm using scrubbers. Table 5.10 illustrates this.

TABLE 5.10 Energy Requirements of Venturi Scrubbers in Iron Founding

Removal efficiency	Energy Requirements (KwH per incremental kilo of particulates removed)
91	1.80
93	1.95
95	2.10
97	4.40
98	7.70
98.5	9.9

Source: Adapted from H Cooper and W Green, Energy Consumption Requirements for Air Pollution Control Equipment in the Iron Founding Industry. Journal of Air Pollution Control, 1978

In the other two industries there are complicating factors of control
for recycling purposes which will prevent any clear cut trade-off
estimates that we have been able to make in the other industries
discussed in this chapter.

CONCLUSIONS

It has been shown that at high levels of control cross-media transfers
of pollution may arise due to the operation of energy intensive pollution
control equipment. The necessary calculations to illustrate the trade-
offs are relatively simple and using the environmental index derived in
Chapter 8 it is clear that some higher rates of control may actually add
to the total environmental burden rather than subtracting from it.

REFERENCES

1.   U.S. Department of Commerce, Energy Requirements for Air Pollution
         Control in the Primary Aluminium Industry. EPA Publications
         No. PB-264-483, 1977

2.   Energy Requirements for Air Pollution Control in Primary Aluminium,
         U.S. Department of Commerce, Washington, D.C. 1977.

PART II

Methodology of Assessment

CHAPTER 6

Cost-benefit Analysis

INTRODUCTION

Cost-benefit analysis is a technique which has developed over the last two
decades to provide information for social decision-making. Its underlying
philosophy is that all the costs and benefits of a particular action should
be considered, to whosoever in society they accrue. For this reason it is
traditionally a tool of government rather than of the individual economic
unit, since the latter might reasonably be expected to formulate decisions
solely on the basis of costs and benefits incident upon itself. Government,
however, has a responsibility to take account of all costs and benefits
to members of society in formulating its own expenditure policy, and, to an
extent, in regulating the activities of firms and individuals who are not
subject to the same policy constraints as itself.

The undertaking of a cost-benefit study can be divided into a number of
steps. The first of these involves the identification of the alternatives
to be assessed. Most commonly this will involve the undertaking of a
project, or no action at all, but the choice may sometimes be between
different projects, where it has already been decided that one will be
pursued, and the study is to help decide which one yields the greatest
net benefits. In any case, cost-benefit studies invariably involve the
comparison of a finite number of alternatives, so in no way can they in
themselves indicate an optimal solution to a problem characterised by
continuous cost and benefit schedules. Practically speaking, a number of
'representative' strategies may be assessed, in the hope that the one
having the greatest net benefits approximates to an optimal solution. The
second step in the process is the prediction of the consequences associated
with each strategy. For example if a steel plant caused n different ways
of abating its emissions then these should be made explicit with their
related consequences. The third stage of the analysis requires the
attribution of values to the consequences predicted for each alternative,
and it is this process which encounters the most serious conceptual
difficulties. This is, of course, because there may not be a market price
for environmental goods, because they are not market traded, or if there
are market prices then these may be distorted or reflect a disequilibrium
situation, and in this case the prices do not represent the true resource

costs associated with the goods used. It is not the intention of the
authors here to go into detail in these issues which have been adequately
discussed elsewhere both in an environmental and general context.(1)(2)
Should any practitioner wish to become involved in the measurement of costs
and benefits of environmental policies he would need to consult one of the
many books on this subject. Having established a value for items of cost
and benefit at the time they occur, it is still necessary to express these
in terms of a present value and this is an issue which we explore later.

Clearly cost-benefit analysis is applicable to cross media environmental
problems. We concentrate below on determining the information requirements
for effective decision-making, and discuss the viability of the use of
cost-benefit analysis, although recently some important alternative
techniques have been suggested. (3)   Clearly the frequency of incidence
of substantial external costs* involving the environment is a rationale
for the use of social decision making machinery. However, the external
cost of pollution to a particular environmental medium cannot be looked at
in isolation. Abatement policies do not destroy matter, but only convert
it from one form to another, an example being the incineration of solid
waste causing air pollution. The problem is not how to dispose of residuals,
but how to convert them into a form which imposes the least cost on society,
including the cost of transformation. This cost must then be compared at
the margin with the social benefit of the pollution-creation product.

CONCEPTUAL AND PRACTICAL PROBLEMS IN THE EVALUATION OF ENVIRONMENTAL COSTS AND BENEFITS

It has been suggested that there are several obstacles which render the use
of cost-benefit analysis inappropriate for the analysis of certain kinds
of environmental problems. Pearce draws attention to the distinction
between economic effects and biological effects. A good example of a
form of pollution involving economic but not biological effects would be
glass bottles and the cost-benefit framework is capable of incorporating
this kind of externality problem. The complex situation arises where
biological forces are affected by an activity, but the economic effect is
imperceptible.

Such a case would be the emission of cadmium, which above a certain level
of concentration can have very serious health implications. In reality,
of course, there is an economic effect associated with such an emission,
but it may well go unperceived, due to the fact that damages emanate from
the stock of pollution, rather than its flow. In the case of wastes
which are essentially non-degradable, any addition to the stock of
pollution imposes a damage cost for an indefinite period into the future,
and this is difficult to ameliorate. Since the cost-benefit framework is
designed to relate damage estimates to flows of pollution, it cannot easily
be adapted for situations where it is the stock of waste that is the
relevant concept, unless the damage from the stock pollutant is valued at
infinity.

---

* An external cost or 'externality' is defined as a cost which is
imposed on an outside party who has no control over the imposition
of the cost. (e.g. smoke from a chimney polluting the air)

A separate, but somewhat related conceptual difficulty occurs where an excess discharge of waste impairs the assimilative capacity of the environment. This is referred to as a 'dynamic externality'. The problem here is that, given the assumption of instantaneous assimilation of waste which is within the environment's capacity, external costs only occur above this level. If there are net private benefits to production above this level, and the marginal external cost curve is upward sloping and continuous, then some level of waste emission above assimilative capacity must be deemed optimal.

If exceeding the environments natural capacity impairs established degrader populations - and thus the assimilative capacity of the environment - then future generations will be able to discharge less and less to various environmental media and optimal production levels (where marginal external cost equals marginal private net benefit) will tend to fall towards zero. Clearly unless the external environmental cost function includes an element for the loss of assimilative capacity then equating costs and benefits as a guide to public decision making will inevitably lead to incorrect decisions. Ignoring discounting considerations this means that the optimum production level for society will be equal to that level which does not breach the assimilative capacity of the environment. Two caveats can however be made. Firstly, if society wishes to use a positive discount rate in its evaluation; then pollution levels in excess of what the environment can absorb will be justified. Secondly, if it is conjectured that future new technology will enable a cleaning up of the environment to a greater extent than is now possible, then clearly the use of a positive discount rate is wholly justified and breaches of the assimilative capacity can be allowed in the short run.

Alternatively it might be equally justifiable to assume a negative rate of discount for future cash flows. As time passes, and manufacturing processes throughout the world become increasingly extensive, environmental resources can be expected to become increasingly scarce and valuable. To treat air and water quality improvements in say, fifty years time as virtually valueless, which is the impact of discounting, seems absurd. This is not to say that equal monetary benefits in different years should always be treated equally. If there are good reasons for valuing benefits accruing at a particular time more highly than others, then there is no theoretical objection to weighting these years individually. For example, if technological advance was expected to develop a pollution-free process for a particular industry in ten years time, then the benefits of a treatment facility for the industry should be weighted to give low values for those accruing after this time. It is the 'straight line' treatment to flows of costs and benefits given in discounting, which is the subject of the valid objection.

It is probably true to assert that the reason discounting has been utilised so unquestioningly in environmental studies, is that without its use, cost-benefit analysis may sometimes lose its relevance. Many activities result in flows of costs or benefits lasting for an indefinite time period, which if summed without discounting have an infinite present value. This may render cost-benefit analysis superfluous to decision making. Conversely, the convenient use of an arbitrary discount rate results in the present value tending to a finite sum, allowing a neat comparison of costs and benefits. The fact that total environmental destruction in, say, two hundred years' time would be minutely valued by this method, does not seem to matter. However, despite the conceptual limitations cost-benefit analysis can usefully be employed for examining many projects and strategies concerned with the environment.

The practical problems of measuring both costs and benefits are substantial, particularly in the case of the latter. In the case of benefit estimation not only has environmental damage (to human health, wildlife, buildings etc) to be measured but the value of this in hard cash has to be estimated as well. This is particularly problematical with human life for instance. Nevertheless attempts have been made and these are adequately documented in Lowe and Lewis (4) for instance. Of equal importance but frequently ignored are some of the attempts to measure costs of control.

There are several aspects of these studies and the data generated which are important. Firstly, there is a very high degree of variability even within very specific industries. In part this is because some of the most heavily impacted industries are those which have a mix of modern and old plant, which means the type of control and user needs will vary. Also locations are different and for a variety of economic, environmental, technical and political factors this may affect the costs of control and the degree of control achieved.

The size of firm and extent of integration also appear to be a determining factor of control costs since large and/or integrated operations which have substantial head office research resources are frequently better placed to negotiate and implement environmental control. This factor has been reinforced in some recent research which found, for instance, that the extent of recycling and firm size were closely linked in the Textile Dyeing and Finishing Industry.(5) There is considerable evidence too of economies of scale existing in the operation of pollution control equipment. This, coupled with the technological problems faced by small firms, means that environmental control may force some firms to merge or go out of business altogether.

However, perhaps the most important aspect of costs is the marginal cost function. Here recent research (6) shows that control at levels much higher than at present, may in some industries lead to very substantial cost increases. One example quoted was in secondary lead processing where it was estimated that for an average plant the total cost of control per tonne of lead produced increased from £2 per tonne at 95 per cent collection efficiency, to £4 per tonne at 99 per cent, to £8 per tonne at 99.8 per cent and £10 per tonne at 99.9 per cent. Ultimately these costs have to be borne by the consumer in the form of higher prices, or shareholders and labour in the form of lower dividends and fewer jobs. Consequently there are important multiplier effects of environmental control which can clearly impact important facets of the economy such as economic growth, unemployment and in some cases international competitiveness.

Several attempts have been made to compare both the costs and benefits of control but the most recent is documented in a OECD study on sulphur oxides. This research did not merely do a cost minimisation exercise as several earlier studies had done. Some attempt at benefit quantification was made - for instance computing the value of fish stocks and crops saved through pollution control. However no attempts were made to value human life or the damage pollution causes to old buildings etc. The former omission, in particular, is important since the recent research both in the U.K. and U.S. (7) (8) on the impact of air pollution on mortality suggests some sensible estimates can be made.

The OECD exercise set out to compare the implication of three scenarios
of air pollution control in eleven European countries. They began by
calculating a reference case the sulphur oxide emissions to be expected
by 1985 without further pollution controls than those already planned.
They then calculated the value of two alternative control strategies one
in which all European countries devoted 0.05% of their gdp to pollution
control and another in which they spent enough to apply the best available
technology. In the reference case, it was reckoned that sulphur-oxide
emissions would rise 21% over their 1974 levels by 1985; in the second
case, they would remain broadly unchanged; and, in the third, they would
drop by 37%.

This naturally involved some forecasting of energy requirements and energy
pollution output ratios, but generally the data seemed relatively good.
This data was then compared to benefit estimates and a summary of some of
the results is given in Table 6.1 below. This shows benefits and costs
broadly in balance and represents one of the first real attempts to
evaluate a programme of air pollution regulations.

The study took the OECD three years to complete for an already well
researched pollutant. Clearly the problems of applying a similar analysis
to less well researched or more diffuse pollutants would be substantial.
However the OECD study is useful if only because it shows how traditional
techniques of economic analysis are (and should) be used in environmental
management.

        CONCLUSION

It has been argued that the inclusion of the costs and benefits of
environmental quality are essential to social decision-making, because
almost all productive activities influence the environment in some way.
Furthermore the residuals arising from these activities can only be
transformed, not destroyed. In the context of the environment, the
predominant role of cost-benefit analysis is to make assessments of the
value to society as a whole of alternative strategies towards the transformation of waste products, in terms of the benefits from environmental
improvement and the costs from the usage of scarce resources.

The measuring rod of money is generally adequate so far as the valuation
of the resource costs of achieving a particular environmental improvement
is concerned, but is often inadequate as a yardstick for the magnitude of
the benefit to society arising from the improvement. This is the explanation
for the observable fact that so many of the larger scale cost-benefit
studies undertaken in the field of the environment have concerned themselves
with determining the most efficient or least cost means of attaining a
particular level of environmental quality, rather than comparing alternative
quality cost configurations.

It would be wrong to infer from the undoubted existence of conceptual and
practical difficulties in the evaluation of environmental benefits that no
useful monetary estimates can ever be made of the benefit to society of a
particular reduction in pollution. In some cases reasonable 'proxies'
are available for benefit measurement, and in others it may be possible to
assess the benefits by dividing them into components. Even where
particular components of benefit are being estimated, valuations can only
be made directly for material damage reduction and production benefits.
In all other cases, values must be inferred from the behaviour of individuals

TABLE 6.1 Costs and Benefits of Sulphur Oxide Control in Eleven European Countries

	Emissions held at 1974 levels			Emissions reduced by 37%		
	Cost	Benefit	Ratio	Cost	Benefit	Ratio
France	385	234–2157	1.6	624	462–4545	1.4
West Germany	257	304–3289	0.8	516	581–6821	0.9
Britain	202	173–949	1.2	650	431–2172	1.5
Holland	88	55–560	1.6	247	138–1244	1.8
Sweden	70	25–126	2.8	155	45–264	3.4
Austria	40	7–153	2.4	100	38–406	2.6
Belgium	38	51–521	0.5	185	113–1075	1.6
Denmark	34	16–118	2.1	94	35–252	2.7
Switzerland	25	20–245	1.3	25	42–543	0.6
Finland	23	3–14	7.7	92	10–48	9.2
Norway	8	6–36	1.3	14	12–81	1.2
Total	1170	904–8168	1.3	2702	1907–17452	1.4

Source: The Costs and Benefits of Sulphur Oxide Control, OECD, 1981

However, so far as choices involving matters of aesthetic improvement or recreational provisions are concerned, there seems to be no reason for supposing that the preferences revealed by individuals are anything other than a true measure of the benefit derived. Unfortunately the same assertion cannot be made for other categories of environmental benefit, in particular improvements in human health.

The basic problem arises from a lack of understanding and knowledge of the health effects of particular pollutants in differing concentrations. The effects on health of certain substances in the air and in water has been estimated by medical researchers, but by laymen most aspects of this subject are very poorly understood. A similar argument would apply to long-term damage of all types arising from the ecological implications of certain types of pollutant. For this reason, it is suggested here that the inference of values for human health from the observed behaviour of individuals is wholly inappropriate. The reasoning is not paternalistic in character. If members of society had sufficient knowledge and under-standing of the complex technological interactions involved, then their revealed preferences would be an appropriate measure of benefit. It is only because of this undeniable information deficiency that these preferences are not meaningful. The implication of this must be that existing benefit evaluation relying on estimates of material damage or inferred behaviour must be replaced by a different type of measure.

Clearly traditional cost benefit analysis has economic potential in helping the formulation of public policy towards cross media transfers. However, real problems exist in its practical implementation as we have discussed above. Consequently in the next chapter we examine an alternative approach to cost benefit evaluation which is particularly suitable for those cases where comparisons have to be made between controls which differentially impact different media.

REFERENCES

1. Lowe, J.F. and Lewis, D.C. 'Economic Approaches to Environmental Decision Making' OMEGA, Vol 7, No.5, pp 421-430
2. Lowe, Julian and Lewis, David. The Economics of Environmental; Management. Philip Allen, 1980
3. Lowe, Julian and Lewis, David. Environmental Choice and Public Decision Making. OMEGA, Vol. 9 No. 3, pp 297-305
4. Lowe, Julian and Lewis, David. The Economics of Environmental Management. Philip Allen, 1980
5. Lowe, J.F. and Atkins, M.H. Resource Conservation and Environmental Control. Resources Policy, Vol.4, January 1978
6. Atkins, M.H. and Lowe, J.F. The Economics of Pollution Control in the Non-Ferrous Metals Industry. Pergamon Press, 1979

7. Atkins, M.H., Lowe, J. and Lewis, D. Air Pollution and Human Health:
    A case study of Environmental Benefit Estimation. International
    Journal of Environmental Studies. 1980. Vol.16, pp 29-34
8. Lave, L. and Seskins, E.P. Air Pollution and Human Health.
    Science, August 1970, p 723.

CHAPTER 7

An Alternative Approach to Cross-media Evaluation

THE RATIONALE FOR USING A 'DELPHI' TECHNIQUE

It is the intractability of the problem of determining the environmental effects of different pollutants that might result from alternative pollution control strategies in some industries, which renders the inference of values from behaviour inappropriate. The whole area is characterised by an ignorance of the real implications of pollutant emissions by the general public, which is not in any way alleviated by the periodic concentration of the mass media on the particular and rather arbitrarily determined adverse effects of one individual form of pollution. Furthermore, the subject of the environmental effects of various pollutants, especially the human health effects, is one in which no one person can have overall expertise. There are many individuals whose knowledge of the effects of certain categories of pollutant emissions could not be challenged, but none who could claim expertise in all the aspects of this very diverse and complex area of study.

A technique has been developed in the United States which appeared to us to offer considerable potential for a partial resolution of the problem of attaching relative valuations to the effects of different pollutants - albeit not in monetary terms. This is the so-called 'Delphi' technique, originally developed as an aid to technological forecasting, but subsequently used in a number of different contexts. Its' base is the anonymous assembly of a panel of individuals, whose expertise varies over the whole sphere of the topic under consideration. The technique is quite separate, both in objective and in concept from the use of more traditional environmental indices.

After a sufficient number of expert individuals have agreed to participate the 'Delphi' exercise is conducted by asking these people the desired questions in the form of a postal questionnaire. The replies are then disseminated and a feedback document containing a synthesis of the views expressed by all participants is sent to each panel member. The precise content of the feedback will depend upon the nature of the topic being pursued, but where a relative valuation of different items is involved, it would normally include mean or median values attached to these items, as

73

well as a list of categorised comments. Respondents are then asked to
confirm or amend their previously expressed views in the light of this
information. It is to be hoped that they confirm those opinions held
strongly, whilst amending those held only tentatively or which are outside
their area of expertise.

The 'Delphi' technique is especially suitable for analysing problems
characterised by an inability for any one person to "command sufficient
technological expertise to unilaterally develop solutions to complex
problems".(1)   One advantage of the technique is that it allows a
meaningful debate to ensue without the necessity to build interpersonal
relationships thus allowing the whole attention of participants to be
focused on the task in hand. It also avoids the phenomenon of group
domination by individuals with big reputations or extrovert manners,
which so often occurs in the conventional 'meeting' situation.
Additionally it allows a group of experts to think through a problem
without any externally imposed time constraints.

Because of these potential advantages, it was decided to use a 'Delphi'
type technique in order to attach relative weightings to emissions of
different pollutants, some to air, some to water and some to land. Such
an exercise was attempted in the United States by Battelle Columbus
Laboratories, (2) but so far as we are aware, no such method has
previously been tried in the U.K.

THE BATTELLE COLUMBUS APPROACH TO POLLUTANT WEIGHTINGS

The development of a methodology for evaluating the environmental impacts
of differing pollution control technologies by means of an index was
attempted by Battelle Columbus Laboratories as an alternative to attaching
meaningless monetary values to levels of environmental improvement. The
approach was to compare a number of possible pollution control alternatives
for a particular productive process, this comparison being in terms of
environmental effectiveness, but with cost figures also specified. An
"Environmental Degradation Index " (E.D.I.) was calculated for each
alternative and the "Strategic Effectiveness Index" (S.E.I.) of a
particular control method was defined as the difference between its 'E.D.I.'
and the 'E.D.I.' of the uncontrolled process (which would normally be
higher.) Thus:-

$$\text{'S.E.I.'}_i = \text{'E.D.I.'}_u - \text{'E.D.I.'}_i$$

where i refers to the ith control strategy and u to the uncontrolled case.

The major innovation in this work was associated with the calculation of
the appropriate 'E.D.I.'s which necessarily involved a subjective relative
valuation of emissions to different environmental media. The method
adopted was to develop two levels of weights, one for comparing different
pollutants within the same medium, and the other level for comparing
damage to one medium with damage to another in general. At each level
the weights were determined by asking a panel of experts to make relative
valuations using a 'Delphi' type process. When, after two or three stages,
a reasonable level of consensus among participants was obtained, these
values were used in the final analysis. For the comparison of pollutants
each panel member was asked to rank a list of pollutants, and then to
rate the second as a fraction in importance of the first, the third of the
second and so on. The weighting of pollutants within a particular medium

was repeated quite separately for each industry considered, whereas it was only necessary to undertake the relative weighting of air, water and land once.

The weighting of pollutants within each medium was undertaken without reference to any specific level of emissions. In order to relate the weightings to different emission levels of each substance resulting from alternative control methods, the concept of a 'maximum' level of emission of each pollutant in a particular industry was introduced. This 'maximum' would be the level of emission in the uncontrolled case, or the highest level arising from any control device under consideration if any of these resulted in an increase in the emission of the particular pollutant — as would occur, for example, where a wet arrestment device caused the creation of a waterborne pollutant.

For each alternative control device the production of each pollutant would be at or below the 'maximum' level. An 'S' shaped damage function was rather arbitrarily assumed, with a damage (dp) varying between 0 and 1 where dp = 1 would apply to the 'maximum' mass emission and dp = 0 to nil emission. Before the dp for each pollutant was multiplied by the two levels of weightings, it was subjected to a so-called 'modifier' designed to reflect the dispersal range, the persistence and the transferability of each pollutant. For example, a substance with a long dispersal range, long persistence, and which is readily transferable would have a 'modifier' value of 0.8, the maximum, whereas the minimum would be 0.1. This 'modifier' was determined entirely independently of the weightings derived from the views of the experts.

Although both levels of weights were determined by use of the 'Delphi' technique, there were differences in the underlying assumptions. In the first place a group of experts was invited to rank and weight pollution to each of the three environmental media (air, water and land). These weights were then 'normalised' so that they sum to 1,000. A group of experts then ranked and weighted a list of air pollutants arising in the particular industry being considered, whilst other groups did the same for the relevant water pollutants and solid waste pollutants. The final weighting was arrived by distributing the overall weighting for air pollution arrived at in the first stage amongst all air pollutants in proportion to the relevant weightings attached to them at the second level, the same procedure being followed for water and solid pollutants. In this way all pollutants pertaining to the industry under consideration would be relatively weighted, the sum of these weights being 1,000.

Using this information, together with data on the mass of emissions of each substance from any individual pollution control strategy, the "Environmental Degradation Index" resulting from each strategy was computed. The formula used was:-

$$EDI_i = \sum_{p=1}^{n} \left[M_p \times dp,i \times w_p \right]$$

where   i is the ith control strategy
          p = 1......n, represents the n pollutants relevant to the industry,
          M_p is the 'modifier' for each pollutant,
          dp,i is the damage from each pollutant resulting from the use
               of the ith strategy, obtained from an 'S' damage function
               and $(0 \leqslant dp,i \leqslant 1)$

and Wp is the weight for each pollutant obtained from the two-level 'Delphi' procedure.

Naturally the lower the 'E.D.I.' emanating from the control device, the more effective it is in overall environmental terms. The larger the difference between the 'E.D.I.' with the control and the 'E.D.I.' without any controls, then the larger is the "Strategic Effectiveness Index" (S.E.I.) for the control. Of course it is possible that where a control device transfers a substantial mass of damaging residuals to another medium its 'E.D.I.' could actually be higher than for the uncontrolled case, making the 'S.E.I.' negative.

The final stage of the Battelle Columbus work involved the presentation of the information derived. This took the form of tabulating for each alternative control strategy the 'S.E.I.', the capital and operating costs of the equipment, and its energy requirement. The objective was both to evaluate the relative effectiveness of different controls, and to compare them in terms of value for money. The two actual processes to which the methodology was applied were the power generation industry (1,000 MW coal-fired plants) and kraft pulp mills (1,000 tons/day capacity).

THE DELPHI TECHNIQUE : OUR OWN EXPERIMENT

It appeared to the present authors that the Battelle Columbus approach provided an interesting and potentially useful alternative to Cost Benefit Analysis for analysing the relative effectiveness of pollution control alternatives in a particular industry. However, there were a number of aspects of the work which seemed unsatisfactory, and whilst we did not have the resources available to a large organisation, we felt it worthwhile to conduct an experiment in the U.K. in order to test the feasibility of incorporating some improvements into the framework of a 'Delphi-type' technique. Some comments are made in the following paragraphs on those aspects of the study which were particularly open to methodological criticism, together with a description of the improvements which we suggest and have tested in our own experiment.

The use of a so called 'modifier' was justified in the American work on the grounds that certain aspects of the behaviour of pollutants in the environment (dispersal range, persistence and transferability) are determinable in an objective way. In order to avoid double-counting it would have been necessary for the experts, when making their weightings, to be instructed specifically to ignore these factors. Our own view is that a wholly subjective approach to valuation is quite appropriate for the reasons outlined in the foregoing sections, and that it is preferable to retain the subjectivity, rather than arbitrarily divide the problem up into subjectively and objectively determinable parts. One would have thought that the three factors included in the 'modifier' were just as subject to differences in opinion as are some considerations excluded from the 'modifier'. The whole rationale for the Delphi approach is that subjective assessments are the only useful ones in this particular area, so in our own experiment we dispensed with the 'modifier' and asked participants to include consideration of dispersal range, persistence and transferability, along with any other factors relevant to damage potential, in their weightings of each pollutant.

The Battelle Columbus study made the assumption of an 'S' shaped damage
function, between the levels of nil emission and the 'maximum' level
described above. The obvious corollary of this is that all pollutants
have their highest marginal impact at a mass emission of about half the
'maximum' for the particular industry concerned. Whilst the postulation
of an S shaped damage function is itself quite plausible, the assumption
that the S shaped characteristics of a particular pollutant manifest
themselves within a range determined only by the emissions of the
substance within one industry is quite unrealistic. The 'maximum' level
of Sulphur Dioxide emitted by a power station would be much higher than
the 'maximum' emission level from, say, a steelworks, and the damage
function at the two levels would presumably be very different.

In order to overcome this conceptual difficulty, we decided to ask our
panel of experts a series of questions for each pollutant, designed to
indicate the form which the damage function for each substance might take.
This seemed to be an improvement over assuming an S shaped function
between nil emissions and a level determined separately for each industry
without direct relation to any meaningful concept of a maximum possible
level of damage. These questions were sent to participants with the first
round of the Delphi correspondence, which is reproduced in the Appendix.

This approach necessitated the use of a specified mass emission of each
pollutant as the basis on which experts were asked to make relative
valuations. The damage potential of a particular mass of any of the
pollutants considered could then be computed by multiplying the pollutant
weight derived from the Delphi process by an index number reflecting the
damage function.

An important consideration in the formulation of our methodology was that
weightings should be based on assumptions which would allow experts to
consider the problem in the most readily comprehensible form. We therefore
specified an emission rate of 100 lb/hr for each of the eight airborne
pollutants, six solid pollutants and all but one of the twelve waterborne
pollutants. For obvious reasons a mass emission rate was not appropriate
for the waterborne pollutant 'Heat' for which an emission of
10^8 B.T.U./hr was specified. It was felt that the use of identical mass
emissions for each substance would assist participants in making
comparisons, and imperial rather than metric units were used as many
people - even some scientists - still find it easier to think in these
terms.

Having specified an emission rate of 100 lb/hr as the basis for relative
pollution weightings, the questions designed to give an indication of the
form of the damage function were formulated with reference to this mass
emission. Participants were asked to estimate what proportionate damage
would be done by 10 lb/hr and 50 lb/hr, and how many times as much damage
would be done by 1,000 lb/hr and 10,000 lb/hr, as compared to that done
by 100 lb/hr. These questions were asked for all eight airborne pollutants,
and all waterborne pollutants except 'Heat'. Details of the precise
formulation are shown in the Appendix. The index number reflecting the
damage function, by which the pollutant weight would be multiplied, would
be less than (or equal to) 1 for any emission of less than 100 lb/hr,
and greater than (or equal to) 1 for larger mass emissions, its precise
value depending upon the damage function estimated for the individual
pollutant by the dissemination of experts' replies to the questions

described. A 'straight line' damage function was assumed for 'Heat' and for all solid pollutants.

Our final major departure from the previous work of Battelle Columbus Laboratories was the use of a single level of weights rather than the two level procedure described above. It is very doubtful whether anyone can meaningfully be asked to relatively value air, water and solid pollution without reference to any particular pollutants. The importance of damage will depend upon the substances emitted and their quantities. It is also questionable whether the policy of dividing the overall weighting for air, water and land amongst individual pollutants which are emitted to each by a particular industry, can be justified. For these reasons, we used a weighting procedure based solely upon the relative valuation of a single list of pollutants. This list was selected in order to include the most important pollutants emitted to each medium in a national context, as well as some specific to those industries to which we apply our methodology.

In pursuance of our wish to present choices to experts in the most meaningful and readily comprehensible form possible, the document sent to them specified some assumptions upon which all relative valuations were to be based. The location was an urban area of the U.K. in which a number of named industries were present. All airborne emissions were at given stack height and given concentrations in p.p.m. or gm/m^3, and waterborne emissions were direct to a non-tidal section of river with a specified flow rate in Million Litres/Day (imperial equivalents being stated in each case). The chemical condition of the river in terms of the D.O.E. classification was given as Class 2. Solid wastes were assumed to be deposited on licensed sites, or otherwise disposed of in the most appropriate way, and sludges were defined as suspensions of solids in excess of 2%.

Of course the selection of an appropriate panel of experts to participate in our 'Delphi' type experiment was of critical importance to the whole analysis. Of over twenty eminent individuals originally contacted, a final sample of 10 agreed to participate and completed their first round documents. In view of the fact that about an hour's completion time on two or more occasions was promised to participants in our introductory letter, and all those invided were individuals whose personal time values would be very high, we considered the response rate to be quite good. It was especially encouraging that a 100% response was received at the second round stage, enabling us to maintain the sample size at 10. Our exercise was by nature an experiment in the operation of a methodology, rather than an attempt to establish definitive values for the damage caused by different pollutants, so that this sample was quite adequate.

Although it is an important part of the 'Delphi' technique that assurances are given to participants regarding their anonymity, it is appropriate to indicate the occupations and status of those who participated. These can be summarised as below. It can be seen that this panel includes members whose expertise is chiefly in the area of one of the three media, as well as some who are expert in topics which encompass the effect of pollution in more than one medium.

Occupation	No	Main Area Of Expertise
Public Servant responsible for environmental protection	l	Air
Senior member of Medical Research Team	l	Air
Executive responsible for Pollution Control at large U.K. Company	l	Air
Senior Technical or Scientific Officer in Water Industry	3	Water
County Council Officer responsible for regulation of tipping (including toxic wastes)	l	Land
Retired Senior Civil Servant	l	
Consultant Chemical Engineer	l	
Professor of Economics with technical knowledge of pollution problems	l	

Participants were initially sent a document listing twenty-six pollutants, together with a short explanation of our research methodology, instructions concerning the method of making weightings, and a list of assumptions. They were asked to rank the pollutants 1-26 in descending order of damage potential, and then to express each of those ranked 2-26 as a percentage in importance of the substance ranked l. All replies were then tabulated and the median percentage for each pollutant was calculated and 'normalised' so that the substance with the highest median was allocated a value of 100%. These median values were displayed alongside the individual's valuations in the second round document sent to experts, which also included a stylised (and anonymous) reproduction of the comments which were made on the initial reply, in response to our invitation for brief remarks by experts in explanation of their weightings. Participants were invited to confirm or amend each weighting in the light of this information. The second round replies showed a significant movement towards a consensus, described more fully below, so that the weightings derived at this stage were taken as final for the purpose of their application to alternative pollution control strategies (reported in Chapter 8).

Our methodology incorporates four essential changes from that previously reported. Firstly we have dispensed with the use of a 'modifier' and made the determination of relative weights wholly subjective, rather than attempting to estimate dispersal range, persistence and transferability objectively. Secondly we have tried to use expert advice in order to make some outline sketch of the damage function for air and water pollutants, instead of making the rather arbitrary assumption of an S shaped form over the relevant range. Closely allied to this strategy is our third refinement, involving asking experts to make comparisons on the basis of specific (and identical) quantities of pollutants, rather than invoking the nebulous concept of the general damage potential of a substance. It is our opinion that this change is especially beneficial in arriving at meaningful relative valuations.

The substitution of single level for 2 level weights has an advantage quite separate from the need to conduct the weighting only once rather than for each individual industry. This is that it now becomes possible to compare the effectiveness of a control measure in one industry with a

measure in a different industry in terms of Strategic Effectiveness, since
the same index numbers are used for each, given that the pollutants
relevant to each industry have been included in the original list. In
principle at least, this might assist a central agency in deciding which
industry could most cost-effectively be required to reduce pollution, if
some overall emission reduction in a particular locality was to be made.
It was not the primary objective of our experiment to make this sort of
comparison, though the possibility of using our methodology in this way
does appear worthy of further consideration.

Our own methodology can be specified as follows:

$$S.E.I._i = E.D.I._u - E.D.I._i$$

where i refers to the ith control strategy and u to the uncontrolled case.

$$E.D.I._i = \sum_{p=1}^{n} \left[d_{p,i} \times w_p \right]$$

where i is the ith control strategy
     p = 1.....n, represents the n pollutants relevant to the industry
     $d_{p,i}$ is the damage from each pollutant resulting from the use
       of the ith strategy. This is obtained by applying the
       quantity of each substance to its damage function, obtained
       in the way described above. Emissions of less than 100 lb
       will have a value of less than (or equal to) 1, whilst
       emissions above this level will have a value greater than
       (or equal to) 1.

     w_p is the weight for each pollutant obtained by the single-level
       Delphi procedure described above.

The results of the 'Delphi' type experiment are outlined below.

RESULTS

It is not intended to suggest that any of the results presented below -
or the application of them to different control measures in some industries,
described in Chapter 8 - are in any sense definitive. We have tested
the feasibility of arriving at meaningful relative weightings for different
pollutants in accordance with our own methodology, and in Chapter 8 we test
the practicability of applying these values to specific choice situations
in a number of industries. In any case our results are location specific
and, for example, the specification of a smaller river to which waterborne
pollutants were discharged would presumably have resulted in higher
relative weights being attached to these emissions. Results are reported
here purely for the purpose of illustrating our methodology, and
demonstrating the kind of output which is capable of being generated by
work in the same vein as our own.

The weightings allocated to each of the 26 pollutants listed at the first
and second round stages are shown in Columns 1 and 2 of Table 7.1. These
are in each case the median values taken from all replies received, this
measure being chosen in preference to the arithmetic mean in order to
eliminate the influence of extreme observations upon the result, which
could be of considerable importance in an exercise such as the one here
undertaken, where a particular expert may have little knowledge of one

TABLE 7.1   Median Weights Allocated by Experts

Pollutant	First Round	Second Round	Difference	Difference as % of 1st reply
Ammonia (A)	32.39	33.69	1.3	4.01
Fluorides (A)	77.74	84.22	6.48	8.34
Heavy Metals (A)	106.01	110.61	4.6	4.34
Hydrogen Sulphide (A)	61.25	62.89	1.64	2.68
Nitrogen Oxides (A)	41.22	47.73	6.51	15.79
Total Organics (A)	42.99	44.92	1.93	4.49
Particulates (A)	42.40	44.92	1.93	4.49
Sulphur Dioxide (A)	58.89	57.83	(1.06)	(1.80)
Ammonia (W)	44.17	42.11	(2.06)	(4.66)
Fluorides (W)	29.45	30.88	1.43	4.86
Heavy Metals (W)	69.49	70.19	0.7	1.01
Suspended Solids (W)	25.91	21.34	(4.57)	(17.64)
Oil and Grease (W)	44.17	44.92	0.75	1.70
Nitrates (W)	25.91	24.71	(1.2)	(4.63)
Phenols (W)	50.06	47.73	(2.33)	(4.65)
Phosphates (W)	22.38	21.34	(1.04)	(4.65)
Cyanides (W)	94.23	95.45	1.22	1.29
Sulphates (W)	12.96	9.55	(3.41)	(26.31)
Sulphides (W)	50.06	44.92	(5.14)	(10.27)
Heat (W)	13.55	7.86	(5.69)	(41.99)
Fertiliser Sludge (S)	11.78	12.35	0.57	4.84
Iron Founding Sludge (S)	14.13	12.91	(1.22)	(8.63)
Metal Finishing Sludge (S)	13.55	12.35	(1.2)	(8.86)
Gypsum (S)	7.66	6.18	(1.48)	(19.32)
Slag (S)	4.12	4.49	0.37	8.89
Coal Ash (S)	3.53	3.93	0.4	11.33

All weights in Columns 1 and 2 are normalised so that the totals are 1,000 points in each case. All figures in brackets are negative.

small part of the pollution problem. The list of substances is of course not exhaustive, but rather was chosen to include the major pollutants in some of the industries considered in Chapter 8 as well as those occurring most commonly in the U.K. in general. The medians shown have been 'normalised' so that the column totals are 1,000 in each case for the purpose of comparison, though this step makes absolutely no difference to the use of the final weights in the following chapter.

Columns 3 and 4 of Table 7.1 show the difference between first and second round weightings, and this difference as a percentage of the first value, respectively. Since the values sent to all participants with the second stage were those shown in Column 1, this itself cannot explain deviations from these in the second round replies. For this reason the percentage changes (column 4) are for the most part small. In the case of our experiment, we deduced that the increase in the weightings of most air pollutants relative to water pollutants resulted largely from a reproduction of comments of some experts to the effect that the river specified was of sufficient flow to secure a considerable degree of dilution of waterborne emissions. Alternatively this could have been explained by those who rated air pollutants most highly sticking to their views, whereas the experts rating water pollutants highly tended to bow to the opinions of others more easily, because their own opinions were held only tentatively.

Table 7.2 lists the inter-quartile ranges of the replies received at each stage, which are a measure of the degree of consensus attained. They reflect the range over which the middle 50% of replies lie, and have been adjusted to be commensurable with the values in Table 7.1. It can be seen that the extent of consensus increased substantially with the second round replies as had been hoped, showing that many experts were prepared to modify their previously expressed views quite significantly. Of course, differences of professional opinion persisted - one would not have expected anything other than this - but, with the exceptions of Heavy Metals and Cyanides to water, these could not be considered quantitatively excessive, given the nature of the problem.

TABLE 7.2   Inter-Quartile Ranges of Replies

Pollutant	First Round	Second Round
Ammonia (A)	41.0	17.5
Fluorides (A)	46.75	25.0
Heavy Metals (A)	61.75	20.0
Hydrogen Sulphide (A)	70.25	48.0
Nitrogen Oxides (A)	40.0	23.75
Total Organics (A)	31.5	16.5
Particulates (A)	27.25	24.25
Sulphur Dioxide (A)	34.0	23.0
Ammonia (W)	62.25	36.25
Fluorides (W)	55.5	41.0
Heavy Metals (W)	77.0	68.0
Suspended Solids (W)	45.25	30.75
Oil and Grease (W)	61.75	47.75
Nitrates	49.5	47.25
Phenols (W)	55.0	45.0
Phosphates (W)	37.0	34.5
Cyanides (W)	80.0	52.5
Sulphates (W)	40.75	22.0
Sulphides (W)	46.75	29.0
Heat (W)	40.25	21.25
Fertiliser Sludge (S)	16.0	16.0
Iron Founding Sludge (S)	29.75	16.0
Metal Finishing Sludge (S)	46.5	17.5
Gypsum (S)	14.25	8.5
Slag (S)	9.25	8.0
Coal Ash (S)	10.0	5.75
TOTAL	1129.25	745.0

Although no confidence can be expressed as to the precision of the weights derived, and indeed such accuracy was never anticipated, the values extracted from the second round replies seem sufficiently meaningful to be used for the appraisal of alternative control strategies attempted in Chapter 8, given that the work is experimental only. The final weights used in the following work are listed in Table 7.3, and were arrived at simply by rounding the second round medians in order to avoid the appearance of any spurious precision.

TABLE 7.3. Final Weights Used

Pollutant	Final Weight
Ammonia (A)	34
Fluorides (A)	84
Heavy Metals (A)	111
Hydrogen Sulphide (A)	63
Nitrogen Oxides (A)	48
Total Organics (A)	45
Particulates (A)	45
Sulphur Dioxide (A)	58
Ammonia (W)	42
Fluorides (W)	31
Heavy Metals (W)	70
Suspended Solids (W)	21
Oil and Grease (W)	45
Nitrates (W)	25
Phenols (W)	48
Phosphates (W)	21
Cyanides (W)	95
Sulphates (W)	10
Sulphides (W)	45
Heat (W)	8
Fertiliser Sludge (S)	12
Iron Founding Sludge (S)	13
Metal Finishing Sludge (S)	12
Gypsum (S)	6
Slag (S)	4
Coal Ash (S)	4
TOTAL	1,000

As mentioned above, an attempt was made to estimate a damage function for most pollutants by asking experts' opinion on this matter.

Again median values were used to represent the replies, and the results are presented in Table 7.4. The index was set at 1 for emissions for 100 lb/hr, since this was the mass at which relative weightings were made. Clearly, sections of surve with slopes in excess of 45° represent marginal damage greater than that pertaining to the 100 lb/hr level, whereas shallower slopes indicate lower marginal damage.

In the case of two pollutants - Total Organics (A) and Phosphates (W), the
damage function over the relevant range was deemed to be of 'straight line'
form, and this form was also assumed for Heat (W) and all solid pollutants.
These results are used in conjunction with the weightings in the way
described earlier.

TABLE 7.4   Damage Functions

lb/hr	10	50	100	1,000	10,000
Index					
Ammonia (A)	0.1	0.5	1	20	500
Fluorides (A)	0.1	0.5	1	25	900
Heavy Metals (A)	0.1	0.5	1	50	2,000
Hydrogen Sulphide (A)	0.1	0.5	1	100	1,000
Nitrogen Oxides (A)	0.1	0.5	1	100	1,000
Total Organics (A)	0.1	0.5	1	10	100
Particulates (A)	0.1	0.5	1	10	200
Sulphur Dioxide (A)	0.1	0.5	1	20	400
Ammonia (W)	0.1	0.5	1	10	125
Fluorides (W)	0.025	0.5	1	10	100
Heavy Metals (W)	0.1	0.5	1	25	750
Suspended Solids (W)	0.075	0.5	1	10	100
Oil and Grease (W)	0.1	0.5	1	10	175
Nitrates (W)	0.075	0.5	1	10	100
Phenols (W)	0.1	0.5	1	20	1,000
Phosphates (W)	0.1	0.5	1	10	100
Cyanides (W)	0.1	0.5	1	75	1,000
Sulphates (W)	0.05	0.5	1	10	100
Sulphides (W)	0.1	0.5	1	15	300

CHAPTER 8

An Application of the Alternative Approach

SCOPE OF THE ANALYSIS

In order to test the practicability of applying our weighting system to actual decision-making situations, we collected data on three industries consisting of raw residual loads, the residuals arising after the use of a number of alternative control strategies, the energy requirements of each control, and an estimate of the annualised cost of each alternative. This information was then used to assess the overall environmental impact of each alternative, which was compared with the cost (including elements of capital and running costs) incurred in operating the control. The industries selected were Power Generation, Iron and Steel Manufacture, and Iron Founding and these were chosen because we were able to derive data that exhibited a degree of cross-media choice. Neither fertilizer manufacture nor metal finishing was included because, although we were able to collect data on alternative control technologies (particularly in the former case), this was usually part of process differences with substantial recycling elements. This made a clear-cut cross-media evaluation difficult.

An analysis of the control options available for the three industries within the framework of our own methodology follows. However, our index of strategic effectiveness (S.E.I.) is a cardinal measure of the damage potential of different quantities of the twenty six pollutants considered, so that, subject to limitations, it is meaningful to make 'cost effectiveness' comparisons between industries in terms of the environmental degradation avoided per unit of control expenditure. This cardinality occurs because of our sketching of damage functions, so that the relative damage of different quantities as well as different pollutants can be estimated. The extent to which cross-industry comparisons are meaningful within the context of our methodology is discussed below.

It should be stressed that for all the industries discussed below, the emission figures for the various control alternatives are used for illustrative purposes only. Although they are realistic figures, in the case of Power Generation they relate to U.S. plants, and also do not necessarily represent all the practicable control options available. Viewed

TABLE 8.1   1,000 mw Coal-Fired Power Plant - Computations

Part (a)   Raw Residual Loads

	1	2	3	4	5
	Qty (lb/hr)	Index (dp)	Weight (wp)	$dp \times w_p$	'E.D.I.'
Pollutant					
NOx (A)	6,900	690	48	33,120	331.2
SO$_2$ (A)	43,700	1,823	58	105,734	1,057.34
Particulates (A)	88,320	1,853	45	83,385	833.85
Total Organics (A)	120	1.2	45	54	0.54
Suspended Solids (W)					
Heat (W)	(4,600)	46	8	368	3.68
Ash (S)	22,080	221	4	884	8.84
Sludge (S)					'E.D.I.$_u$ =
				223,545	2,235

Part (b)   Control Option (i)

	1	2	3	4	5
	Qty (lb/hr)	Index (dp)	Weight (wp)	$dp \times w_p$	'E.D.I.'
Pollutant					
NOx (A)	6,907	691	48	33,168	331.68
SO$_2$ (A)	43,744	1,825	58	105,850	1,058.50
Particulates (A)	921	9.2	45	414	4.14
Total Organics (A)	120	1.2	45	54	0.54
Suspended Solids (W)					
Heat (W)	(4,605)	46.1	8	369	3.69
Ash (S)	109,589	1,096	4	4,384	43.84
Sludge (S)					'E.D.I. =
				144,239	1,442

in this light, the results presented below appear to indicate encouraging
preliminary evidence of the viability of the kind of analysis suggested.

The means of computation of the Environmental Degradation Inded (E.D.I.)
and Stretegic Effectiveness Index (S.E.I.) is illustrated by reference
to Table 8.1. In each of the three industries considered, tables were
drawn up indicating the quantities of the various pollutants emitted with
each method of control as well as in the uncontrolled case, and Table 8.1
is a reproduction of part of the computation process for the Power
Generation industry. Part (a) shows the residuals arising in the absence
of any control device, whilst part (b) indicates those arising from
the first control option including both residuals which arise despite
the control and new pollutants which arise because of it. Similar tables
(not shown) were compiled for each of the other control options evaluated.
Since the objective of the analysis was to compare alternative strategies,
it was not necessary to include any emissions which are invariant over
the whole range of controls considered.

In Column I the quantities of emissions of each substance are given
in lb/hr (with the exception of Heat). The damage index (dp) shown in
Column 2 is calculated by interpolating from the damage functions of the
particular pollutant which were presented diagrammatically in Figure 7.1.
The pollutant weight (wp) in Column 3 is taken directly from Table 7.3,
and the damage potential of the specific quantity of the particular
substance is computed in Column 4, simply by multiplying Columns 2 and 3.
The 'E.D.I.' is arrived at by summing the various damage potentials, and
dividing by 100 for ease of comparison. The 'E.D.I.'of the uncontrolled
case is referred to as 'E.D.I.$_u$' and the 'E.D.I.'for each control option

is subtracted from this in order to obtain the 'S.E.I.' of the particular
control device. In the case illustrated, the 'S.E.I.' of Control
Option (i) is:-

$$2,235 - 1,442 = 793$$

In the following sections information concerning the 'S.E.I.' cost and
energy requirements of the various alternatives considered are presented
in tabular form, together with an analysis of potential implications.

POWER GENERATION

The basis for comparison in Power Generation is a 1,000 m.w. Coal-Fired
Power Plant, utilising seven alternative types of control device. Table 8.2
presents the basic data computed using our methodology. Since some of the
controls themselves have significant power requirements (column 1), the
final emission quantities for pollutants have been adjusted to take account
of the residuals generated by the production of this extra power. The
annual cost data in Column 2 includes elements of both capital and operating
costs and is in terms of 1973 U.S. dollars. The 'E.D.I.' and 'S.E.I.' are
couched in terms of degradation arising from mass emissions per hour of
plant operation, so comparability requires that cost figures are converted
into these terms, which is done in Column 3. Column 6, representing the
overall effectiveness of the measure per hourly dollar of expenditure, is
a measure of the 'cost effectiveness' of each device.

TABLE 8.2 1000 mw Coal-Fired Power Plant – Data

('E.D.I.'$_u$ = 2,235)

Control Device	1 Energy reqd (mw)	2 $m 1973 ammortised cost per annum	3 $ 1973 cost per hour of plant operation	4 E.D.I.	5 S.E.I. (2,235 – E.D.I.)	6 S.E.I. per hourly $
(i) Electrostatic precipitator – flyash removed dry with bottom ash	1	2.27	270	1,442	793	2.94
(ii) Electrostatic precipitator with sedimentation pond	0	0.79	94	1,441	794	8.45
(iii) Electrostatic precipitator – flyash removed as slurry	1	2.27	270	1,591	644	2.39
(iv) Wet limestone scrubbing	40	21.86	2,602	675	1,560	0.60
(v) Magnesium Oxide scrubbing	40	24.60	2,929	434	1,801	0.61
(vi) 'Cat-ox' scrubbing	40	26.57	3,163	434	1,801	0.57
(vii) Two stage combustion	0	0.08	9.5	2,050	185	19.47

Source: Battelle Columbus Laboratories

It can be quite clearly seen from the data in Columns 5 and 6 that some
devices are more effective than others in overall environmental terms, and
also that some give more potential damage avoidance per unit of remedial
expenditure than others. Magnesium Oxide scrubbing and 'Cat-Ox' scrubbing
appear to be the most effective controls, but are also very costly.
Option (vii) - Two Stage Combustion - is very 'cost effective' but avoids
only a little over 10% of the damage prevented by options (v) and (vi).
Unremarkably, the most effective devices (iv), (v) and (vi) are also shown
to be the most costly per unit of degradation avoided.

The most positive implication of the data computed is that certain options
are shown, within the terms of our analysis, to be unambiguously inferior
to at least one alternative option. Thus option (i) is both less effective
and more costly than option (ii), and the same applies to option (iii)
with respect to (ii), and to option (iv) with respect to (v). This must
call the use of Controls Methods (i), (iii) and (vi) into question, and
any justification for their use in a new plant would have to be on the
basis of some factor other than cost or overall environmental effectiveness.

So far as the remaining four control devices are concerned, the most
revealing indication as to their relative efficacies is obtained by
examining the incremental effects of successively more effective devices
being used, which are shown in Table 8.3. Since the controls are
alternatives, the incremental 'S.E.I.' and cost of a device is its own
'S.E.I.' and cost, less that of the next most effective device, and these
incremental values are given in Columns 1 and 2 respectively. It can be
seen that the first $9.5 expenditure per hour, the cost of device (vii),
secures 19.5 units of environmental improvement per dollar, which is shown
in Column 3. The next $84.5 of expenditure, the cost of substituting
control (ii) for (vii), results in 7.2 units of improvement per dollar,
whilst successively substituting options (iv) and (v) give 0.31 and 0.74
units of 'S.E.I.' per dollar respectively.

Clearly the extent to which environmental improvement should be pursued
given the (for the most part) decreasing returns to scale from successive
expenditures, is a question which cannot be completely answered without
knowing the value to society of units of environmental damage avoided.
However, apart from cross-industry comparisons which are discussed later,
Table 8.3 does give indications as to which controls might be preferable.
Depending upon the level of control desired, then options (vii), (ii) or
(v) might be used. Evidence against the use of options (i), (iii) and
(vi) has been presented and the data would also tend to indicate doubts
about control (iv).

TABLE 8.3 1,000 mw Coal-Fired Power Plant - Analysis

Control Device (see Table 8.2)	1 Incremental 'S.E.I.'	2 Incremental Cost (hourly $ 1973)	3 Incremental 'S.E.I.' per (hourly $ 1973)
(vii)	185	9.5	19.5
(ii)	609	84.5	7.2
(iv)	766	2,508	0.31
(v)	241	327	0.74

Note: Options (i), (iii) and (vi) have been excluded from the above table, because in each case an alternative is available which is both more effective and less costly.

IRON AND STEEL MANUFACTURE

Iron and Steel manufacturing data are based on production at the rate of 300 te/hr, either by one 300 te/hr Basic Oxygen Furnace or by four 75 te/hr Electric Arc Furnaces. Control devices A1 and A2 refer to the former, and B1 and B2 to the latter process. The uncontrolled case, for which 'E.D.I.$_u$' was estimated to be 201, was taken as the raw residuals load on the Basic Oxygen Furnace. Data for the four control options are presented in Table 8.4.

The energy requirements of control devices in iron and steel manufacture are quite considerable, and, as was discussed more exhaustively in Chapter 5, power generation itself produced a significant mass of residuals. In order to assess the overall environmental impact of any control device, the impact of the generation of the energy required to operate it must be included, and this is attempted in Table 8.4. Using data taken directly from Table 8.2 above, and assuming power to be generated at a power station using an Electrostatic Precipitator with Sedimentation Pond for control (corresponding to our Option (ii) in the previous section), the environmental degradation in terms of our 'E.D.I.' caused by the generation of each megawatt of power was 1.44, and this is used to compute the 'E.D.I.' arising from energy which is shown in Column 4.

It should be noted that these figures are only tentative estimates of damage from energy generation, both because a more efficient control device might be used at the power station, and because residuals whose emission is invariant over the whole range of control options were not included in the calculation of the 'E.D.I.' arising from power plants. The 'E.D.I.' from energy figures are added to the data in Column 2, which is an estimate of the 'E.D.I.' arising directly from the particular control device, to give the overall figure shown in Column 5. The information on 'S.E.I.' and 'S.E.I.' per hourly dollar are calculated in the same way as in Table 8.2 for power generation.

TABLE 8.4   300 te/hr Steel Manufacture by Basic Oxygen Furnace (Process A) and Electric Arc Furnace (Process B) Data

Control Device	1 $ 1973 cost per hour	2 E.D.I. after control	3 mw energy required	4 E.D.I. from energy	(5 2+4) Total E.D.I.	6 S.E.I. (201 – total E.D.I.) (E.D.I.$_u$ = 201)	(6/1) S.E.I. per hourly $
A1 Venturi scrubber with hooding and bag filters for building evacuation. Liquid treatment using clarifier, polymer addition and lime precipitation	1,281	27.4	26.2	37.7	65.1	136	0.106
A2 Dry electrostatic precipitator with hooding and building evacuation	1,368	20.1	17.3	24.9	45.0	156	0.114
B1 Baghouse primary and secondary treatment	9,018	3.0	13.7	19.7	22.7	178	0.020
B2 Venturi scrubber with building evacuation also liquid treatment	13,983	8.9	26.5	38.2	47.1	154	0.011

Note: Estimates are based on a 300 te/hr plant for process A, and 4 x 75 te/hr plants for process B

Sources: Chapter 4 and 7

An interesting, though perhaps unsurprising, observation that can be
made from Table 8.4 is that in the case of each device considered, the
degradation from energy generation is greater than the total direct
degradation from the process with the control, and this suggestion of
the importance of energy is supported in our more detailed consideration
of the power requirements of control equipment reported in Chapter 5.   So
far as individual controls are concerned, it can be seen that, whilst
Option Bl is the most effective, both the controls relating to the Basic
Oxygen Furnace provide more units of environmental improvement per dollar
of expenditure, there being little to choose between Options Al and A2 in
this respect.

TABLE 8.5   300 te/hr Steel Manufacture - Analysis

Control Device (see Table 8.4)	1 Incremental 'S.E.I.'	2 Incremental Cost (Hourly $ 1973)	3 Incremental 'S.E.I.' per hourly $ 1973
Al	136	1,281	0.106
A2	20	87	0.230
Bl	22	7,650	0.003

Table 8.5 provides further incremental analysis corresponding to that in
Table 8.3, and Option B2 has been excluded since it is both less effective
and more costly than A2 and Bl.   It can be seen that the highest
incremental 'S.E.I.' per dollar is achieved by substituting control A2
for Al, though this is over the relatively small range of 20 units of
'S.E.I.'   Certainly Control B2 should not be entertained unless there is
some powerful reason for adopting it which is exogenous to our methodology,
and Bl would only seem worthwhile if a very high value is placed on the
extra 22 units of environmental improvement it would accomplish.   Tentative
evidence in favour of using control A2 would seem to be provided by the
analysis.

IRON FOUNDING

The information tabulated for the iron founding industry is based on
production at the rate of 42 te/hr using various combinations of cupolas.
The use of different sized cupolas allows comparisons between controls to
be made within the context of devices which might realistically be applied
to cupolas of a particular capacity.   The alternatives range from twelve
$3\frac{1}{2}$ te/hr to two 21 te/hr cupolas, and are shown in Table 8.6.   The columns
and computations correspond exactly to those applicable to iron and steel
manufacture given in Table 8.4.

As it was observed for iron and steel plants, the 'E.D.I.' arising from
the power requirements of control equipment is quite substantial relative
to total degradation after the employment of controls in the case of all
devices except the simple wet arrester - Option (i).   The most effective
control, the hot-blast cupola with fabric filters, Option (vi), is also
the best value for money in terms of 'S.E.I.' per pound, but the

TABLE 8.6 42 te/hr Multiple Cupola Iron Foundry – Data

Cupolas and Control Device	1 £1978 control control cost per hour of operation	2 E.D.I. after control	3 mw energy required	4 E.D.I. from energy	(2+4) Total E.D.I.	6 S.E.I. (3.84 – total E.D.I.)	(6÷1) S.E.I. per hourly £
12 x 3.5 te/hr cold-blast cupolas with simple wet arresters (i)	65.3	2.43	0.04	0.06	2.49	1.35	0.021
6 x 7 te/hr cold-blast cupolas with dry multicyclone plants (ii)	125.1	1.24	0.23	0.33	1.57	2.27	0.018
3 x 14 te/hr cold-blast cupolas with high efficiency venturi scrubbers (iii)	142.5	1.17	0.67	0.96	2.13	1.71	0.012
3 x 14 te/hr cold-blast cupolas with heat exchangers and fabric filters (iv)	149.6	0.41	0.50	0.72	1.13	2.71	0.018
2 x 21 te/hr hot-blast cupolas with high efficiency venturi scrubbers (v)	121.0	1.17	0.63	0.91	2.08	1.76	0.015
2 x 21 te/hr hot-blast cupolas with heat exchangers and fabric filters (vi)	127.1	0.41	0.47	0.68	1.09	2.75	0.022

Sources: Chapters 4 and 7

differences between the values for each control in Column 7 are
relatively less marked than in either Power Generation or Iron and
Steel manufacture. Options (iii) and (iv) can in any case be discounted
as in both instances a control is available which is both more effective
and less costly.

Table 8.7 is analogous to Tables 8.3 and 8.5, giving an incremental
breakdown of environmental improvement from substituting successively more
effective controls. It is observed that the marginal effectiveness of
devices tends to rise, and that the incremental 'S.E.I.' per £ is greatest
for the substitution of Option (vi) for Option (ii). This analysis would
lend much support to the use of Control technology (vi).

TABLE 8.7   42 te/hr Iron Foundry - Analysis

Control Technology (see Table 8.6)	1 Incremental 'S.E.I.'	2 Incremental Cost (hourly £ 1978)	3 Incremental 'S.E.I.' per hourly £ 1978
(i)	1.35	65.3	0.021 (0.026)
(v)	0.41	55.7	0.007 (0.009)
(iii)	0.51	4.1	0.124 (0.155)
(vi)	0.48	2.0	0.240 (0.300)

Notes:

(1)   Options 3 and 4 have been excluded from the table, because options
      are available which are both more effective and less costly

(2)   Figures in brackets in Column 3 represent an approximate conversion
      factor from £1,978 to $1,973.

CROSS-INDUSTRY COMPARISONS AND CONCLUSIONS

Our methodology has been designed to give a measure of overall
environmental damage, and our 'S.E.I.' is an index of environmental
improvement such that any appropriately measured 'S.E.I.' in one industry
is commensurable with one calculated for the use of a control device in
another industry, provided that all emissions which are not invariant
between the use of the control and the uncontrolled state are of substances
included in the list of pollutants weighted. Thus, given that the most
effective devices considered for Power Generation, Iron and Steel, and Iron
Founding gave 'S.E.I.'s of 1,801, 178 and 2.75 respectively, it is
meaningful to say that the particular device on a power plant avoids
approximately 10 times as much potential environmental damage as the
other particular device on the iron and steel plant, and about 650 times
as much as the control on the iron foundry.

The most interesting comparisons that can be made between different
industries using this methodology involve the incremental units of 'S.E.I.'

per incremental unit of hourly expenditure using the final columns of
Tables 8.3, 8.5 and 8.7. Micro-economic theory tells us that, given a
fixed overall budget for pollution abatement, the greatest reduction
of damage from pollution is obtained by pursuing different controls up
to the level where the damage avoided by them per incremental unit of
expenditure is equal.

An examination of the final columns of these tables would suggest that all
the devices for power generation are more cost effective than any for iron
and steel manufacture, or for iron founding (using an approximate
conversion factor for £1,978 to $1,973), so that a strong case could be
made out for devoting expenditures to the most effective device on a power
plant before spending any resources on controls to iron founding or iron
and steel plants. The relative cost-effectiveness position between iron
and steel, and iron founding devices is more ambiguous. Clearly the
optimal economic solution would be to list controls in all three industries
together in order of descending incremental cost-effectiveness, and to
adopt them in order until the funds devoted for the purpose were exhausted.

Certainly our methodology, given the more sophisticated data as inputs
which could only be achieved by the devotion of resources far in excess
of those available for the present undertaking, would be capable of
providing this information for major industries. Subject to a number of
limitations outlined below, we believe that a methodology such as the one
developed could, on the evidence of our feasibility study, be used as a
tool in decision-making concerning the allocation of resources for
environmental control both within and between industries.

Our analysis in the form presented above does not, of course, include all
factors relevant to a particular decision. Where there are important
considerations exogenous to the computations, these might profitably be
included in the final data presentation in the same way as this is done
in some better cost-benefit studies. Among the factors which might be
important under this heading are distributional effects and the influence
of different decisions on regional and employment policies. Furthermore,
and quite fundementally, unlike cost-benefit analysis the methodology
cannot suggest how much in aggregate should be spent on abatement, but only
how a fixed budget might best be allocated. Finally, a potentially serious
limitation is imposed by the locational specific nature of relative
weightings, implying that cross-industry comparisons are only strictly
justifiable where the different plants are situated in the same area,
though useful indications of relative cost effectiveness will still be
possible in many cases where this condition is not entirely satisfied.

In each of the industries considered above, some indications were given
as to some options which were preferable, and others which were less
preferable. It is emphasised that no firm policy conclusions should be
drawn from these purely illustrative conclusions, since more detailed
data and a rather larger scale Delphi weighting procedure would be
necessary for positive recommendations to be made. Nevertheless it
appears that this feasibility study provides sufficient evidence of the
practicability of this kind of approach for it to be given serious
consideration as an aid to decision-making in the future.

PART III

Public Policy and Conclusions

CHAPTER 9

Comprehensive and Piecemeal Approaches to Control

INTRODUCTION

Ultimately, what really matters with cross media pollution transfers, in the absence of private solutions, is the organisation and instruments of control. This and the next chapter deal with these issues. What constitutes a comprehensive approach to regulation may be somewhat arguable. It is worth recognising that defacto most control agencies with responsibility for a single medium would claim that they do not act recklessly with respect to other media. This may or may not be so, certainly the evidence we received earlier on in this book was rather mixed on this issue. It is likely that the impact on other media is taken into account but ultimately if political and economic pressure persists, a line of least resistance involving cross media transfers to other media may become attractive. The other issue which we do not in fact deal with here, but is of equal importance, is that concerning an agency which is not only comprehensive in the control of the environment but also in terms of the supply of environmental and other goods. Responsibility for public water supply should clearly be under the control of those who protect the water environment. Both control and supply of resources are clearly just as logically linked as controls over various environmental media. This was recognised by Ayres and Kneese (1) whose 'Materials Balance Approach' in its simplest form, recognises the environment as a large shell surrounding the economic system. Raw materials flow from the environment, are processed in the production sector and converted into consumer goods. Residuals are produced in both production and consumption and flow back to the environment unless they are recycled. The environment is thus a provider of material and a receptor and assimilator of wastes. It follows that the lack of a comprehensive approach to the environment will possibly introduce perverse incentives in the system. This is the case within the area of pollution where discharge to one medium may have a different cost:damage ratio to discharge to another. It is also true, however, that the pricing or tax incentives for using virgin raw materials (like water) may introduce a disincentive to recycle.

A COMPREHENSIVE APPROACH

The logic of what we have considered earlier in the book suggests there is
ample justification for seriously considering a unified approach to
pollution. However, from both conceptual and practical points of view
there may be some important caveats. A starting point is to underline that
the real question that the materials balance approach should pose to
economists and policy makers is not <u>whether</u> there are interactions and
linkages (as there clearly are) but <u>whether these are strong enough to
warrant attention</u>. In this respect the evidence is not conclusive on the
extent of cross media problems. It would, of course, from a conceptual
viewpoint, take only a few steps to show that what is needed is a world
agency for everything. This is fine in 'Computoria' but difficult on
'spaceship earth'. Even if we limit our field of vision there are also
uncomfortable alternatives that arise. Water quality depends on water
quantity. Navigation depends on quantity too - as would hydro electric
power. The magnitude of benefits will depend on the recreational and
productive uses of water courses, which rely on quantity and quality. If
all these factors are related, should not they all become the responsibility
of a single authority?

Secondly, a unified control inspectorate justified on the basis of the
materials balance approach should, in theory, have its strategy directed
by the results of benefit evaluation studies, and as we have already
established, this can be something of a difficult area. Certainly this is
so when damage cost ratios between media for various pollutants have to be
established and when the overall level of spending on control is required.

Thirdly, an important feature of the concept of transfers of pollutants is
that of time. Some control strategies effectively delay damage and a
unified approach to control would need to pay particular consideration to
problems of social time preference. It may be argued that this is an
issue that is best dealt with by agencies that are not distanced by large
bureaucracies from the communities they serve. It would be quite appropriate
to apply different rates of discount to different problems in various
locations, yet this is probably something a national unified agency would
have severe political problems in doing. Thus in response to the various
needs for material wealth, employment and a good environment local
communities achieve some desired balance between these goals which in the
past has resulted in vastly different air and water quality conditions
between different areas. This is not inherently sub-optimal but merely
reflects that the environmental and economic systems are entirely interlinked. It is likely that a unified control agency would be under
pressure to achieve much greater homogeneity, which might not actually be
optimal.

A fourth conceptual problem is that there are important contrasts as well
as parallels between the effects and modes of management of air and water
pollution. Air and human health seem likely to be linked but once potable
water supplies have been guaranteed, the damage implications of water
pollution seem to be more connected with aesthetics and recreation. The
modes and methods of control and treatment for air and liquid pollutants
are also often effectively different. Air pollution is difficult to
treat once beyond the 'factory fence' but water pollution is perhaps
easier to treat in these circumstances. Equalisation and neutralisation
of different pollutants and the benefits of large scale economies in
sewage treatment emphasise this.

A final question that must be asked is to what extent does a unified approach to the environment solve the basic environmental problems? If we view these as being mainly concerned with the usage of common property resources, the attendant public good problems, the recognition of the assimilative capacity of the environment as a scarce good, and the design of the tools required to internalise externalities, then it is not at all clear that the reorganisation of agencies into a comprehensive body would in any way achieve anything like the environmental improvement that for instance an effectively operated system of economic incentives would, even if these were based on an ad hoc and piecemeal approach.

It would seem that there is an important conceptual and theoretical basis in favour of a comprehensive approach to environmental control. However, this may be merely a facet of the more general case that everything is interlinked and that a singling out of pollution for comprehensive treatment may not on its own be justified. At the same time there is no reason to believe that a unified approach would solve problems of benefit evaluation, social time preference and adequate control technology any better than a more piecemeal system. Perhaps the basic problem is that economics is better at detecting inefficiency than measuring its extent. Thus whilst we recognise the inherent potential for inefficiency with the current system, ways of evaluating the extent of this are strictly limited.

AN ECONOMIC MODEL

As we are dealing with basically a policy issue it is worthwhile to examine the underlying economic considerations that may be pertinent to the implementation of an environmental control policy concerned with cross-media and intra-media effects.

A natural starting point is an evaluation of the social maximand (social cost optimisation) and possible ways of achieving it. Consider Figure 9.1.

Assume process residuals can be discharged to medium 1 without any private cost but with a MEC shown by MSC_1. There is a constant private cost of discharge to medium 2 (the use of control equipment), and the marginal social cost is shown by MSC_2. If there is no public regulation of emission emissions, firms will produce Q_A, and discharge all residuals to medium 1, for which no cost is incurred. If, alternatively, the only government interference is to insist on the use of a control device which transfers the pollution to medium 2, then Q_B will be produced and all residuals will go to medium 2. The ideal solution, if the firm must discharge exclusively to one medium or the other, is to produce Q_C where emissions are to medium 1, or Q_D if they are to medium 2. This could, of course, be achieved either by an appropriate charge or by government direction.

If it is possible for total discharge to be distributed between the two media, as may be the case where there are numerous firms involved, then the ideal solution will be rather different. In Figure 9.2, the MSC (1 or 2) curve reflects the marginal social cost of successive discharges to either of the media, and is the horizontal summation of MSC_1 and MSC_2. The optimal production is now Q_B, of which OQ_D should

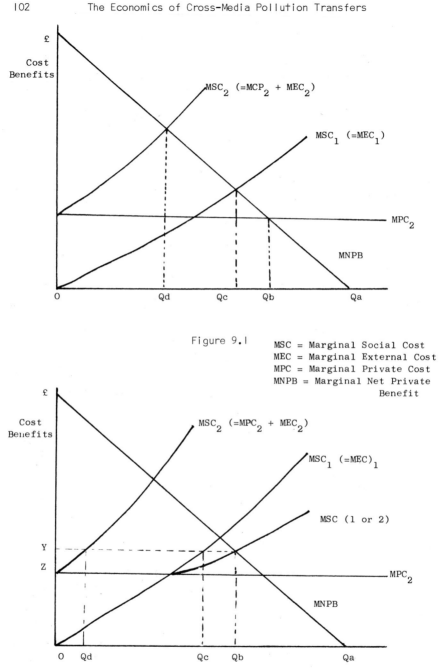

Figure 9.1

MSC = Marginal Social Cost
MEC = Marginal External Cost
MPC = Marginal Private Cost
MNPB = Marginal Net Private
                        Benefit

Figure 9.2

involve emissions to medium 2, and OQ_c to medium 1. This result could
again be achieved either by direct government direction to all firms, or
by appropriate charges for the use of environmental resources. In this
case the charges levied should be OY for a unit discharge to medium 1, and
ZY for medium 2, each of which reflect the marginal damage (or external
cost) caused. A point to notice is that it is the marginal social cost
to each medium which should be equalised for optimality, and not the
marginal damage. Thus it may be quite desirable for higher marginal damage
to pertain for one medium than another, where the latter involves a higher
private cost in emission. Thus public policy should optimise pollution
transfers, not eliminate them.

Having made a number of assertions concerning the ideal solution to problems
of cross media transfers, it is now necessary to consider how these
solutions might be achieved. It would certainly be theoretically possible
for the government to set standards for each firm for each medium, just
stringent enough to force them to reduce emissions to the desired level.
Unfortunately this would require a large volume of information. It would
also have the effect of permitting an amount of pollution to be transferred
without any charge. This latter difficulty could be overcome by
substituting a charge for all emissions to each medium, equivalent to the
marginal damage caused.

Quite apart from any administrative difficulties, both of these solutions
encounter the problem of determining in some way the damage caused at the
margin by a unit emission of residual. A possible solution would be the
auctioning of separate batches of vouchers for each environmental medium.
A system of vouchers would incorporate a standard in the sense that the
total volume of emissions to each medium over a given time period would be
strictly limited to the number of vouchers. Conversely, it would be
equivalent to a charge in the sense that every unit of emitted residual
must be paid for at the market rate for vouchers. There would be an
automatic mechanism for ensuring that the marginal damage of an emission
were not higher than the price paid for vouchers, since any anti-pollution
lobby could enter the market themselves in order to purchase vouchers.
This would have the effect of forcing up the price to the level at which
the damage is valued by society. A problem would undoubtedly arise, in
that unused emission vouchers are a public good, so that the market
mechanics would work efficiently only if this could be overcome by the
intervention of associations, or perhaps local authorities.

This brief discussion of what the social maximand is, and how it could be
achieved, suggests that a unified agency must, in theory, consider both
the costs and benefits of environmental control, if it was to direct the
residual output activity of firms adequately. However, if market solutions
based on economic incentives were to be pursued, then a piecemeal approach,
whereby individual agencies administered centrally agreed limits to total
residual emissions (based on some evaluation of the assimilation capacity
of the environment) would have few disadvantages to a comprehensive one.
If government direction is the chosen 'modus operandi' then benefit
evaluation is, as has already been stated, a necessary feature of a control
agency's information system.

Another economic consideration that arises with a unified agency is that it
could mean vesting all of the nation's environmental resources in the
control of one monopoly body. A full discussion of competition in the
provision of environmental services is outside the scope of this book,

but a few points bear some consideration. Without free choice of different environmental media into which to discharge, individual polluters might have a reduced incentive to search out new processes and control options. In addition the extent to which both charges and standards could be set at excessively high levels would be increased, especially if the monopoly body had some financial incentive to restrict output, or began to over price its resources due to excessive risk aversion, x-inefficiency and organisational slack.

Income distribution is another factor that may need to be considered. Two important points can perhaps be made in this direction. Firstly, recent studies of the distributive impact of environmental control policies suggest they are, if anything, slightly regressive. If this state of affairs necessitates central government subsidies then clearly a unified agency would be an adequate vehicle for this. A unified agency could also be in a better position to sort out the rather anomolous issue of private property rights that can be a distinguishing feature of water resources. It might be suggested that the existence of fishing rights etc. biasses environmental control systems away from using the waterborne media to using the air for discharges of residuals. This is likely to have income distribution effects if, as seems the case, the ownership rights of various water courses are vested in higher income groups whereas lower income groups in urban areas seem likely to suffer the greatest damage from airborne pollutants.

CONCLUSION AND EVALUATION

There may be a good theoretical case for a comprehensive approach to environmental control but any evaluation must also conclude on whether reorganisation is warranted by the actual conditions and deficiencies of the current strategy.

Whilst conceptually it might be expected that a piecemeal approach would lead to an under investment in pollution control the evidence on cross media transfers of pollution does not suggest any unambiguous answers. However, it is really a very difficult issue to judge unless reliable measures of environmental benefit can be calculated. It is a contention of this chapter that until a 'reliable' system of damage evaluation is used there are likely to be few major benefits of changing an existing piecemeal system. The only alternative is to use the cost minimisation approach of those researchers who have looked at cross media issues in the context of the Delaware Valley in the U.S. (2) Refinements of the piecemeal approach may yield a better return, particularly if control agencies concerned themselves with pollutants rather than processes for instance.

REFERENCES

1.   Ayres, R.U. and Kneese, A.V. (1969). Production, Consumption and Externalities. American Economic Review. p.282

2.   Kneese, A.V. and Bower, B.T. (1979). Environmental Quality and Residuals Management. Resources for the Future. John Hopkins, University Press.

CHAPTER 10

Standards and Charges

ECONOMIC ANALYSIS

The debate over standards or charges for environmental pollution control
has centred in recent years on the practicability of the alternative means
of regulation, in terms of the information required for their administration
and the cost of their enforcement. It has been almost universally agreed
that appropriately set charges or standards would in theory be capable of
securing optimal levels of output and pollution control, but that in reality
this ideal solution is confounded by our lack of understanding of the
nature of the environmental damage functions. A frequently canvassed
compromise is to set somewhat arbitrarily determined standards of environmental improvement, but to achieve these standards in the least cost way
to society by means of a uniform charge per unit of emission on all
emitters.

We do not take issue with the apparent consensus of opinion in these matters.
However it is argued that in the 'special case' where there are potential
cross-media transfers of pollution, the effects of imposing standards or
charges which appear to be optimal to the regulators, may be very different
indeed. Furthermore, since this 'special case' is perhaps the rule rather
than the exception in an advanced industrial society, the public policy
implications of the theoretical analysis are discussed.

In order to introduce the tools of analysis, let us consider the simple case
of a productive activity which causes some form of pollution, and where this
can be partially obviated by the employment of a control device. Suppose
that the marginal damage caused by the emissions from the production of
successive units of product, is shown by MD_u in Figure 10.1, but that a
control system is available which reduced this damage to MD_c for different
levels of output. Of course, the relationship between product output and
damage to the environment is a complex and indirect one, involving the mass
of emissions and the ambient air or water concentration of residuals.
Nevertheless the relationship is an important one, and one which is
substantially altered when a control device is introduced.

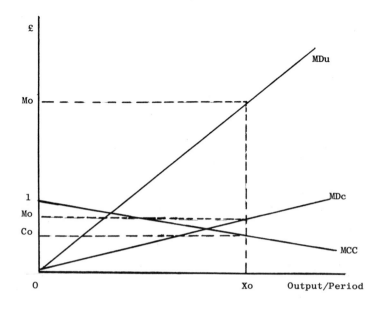

Figure 10.1

Pollution controls often involve real resource costs, both in terms of capital and operating expenditures. In Figure 10.1 the long-run marginal cost of installing and running the control device on successive units of production capacity is shown by MCC. Thus, for example, on a plant manufacturing Xo units of final product per period the uncontrolled marginal damage would be Mo, and this could be reduced to Mo' at a marginal cost of Co - that is, the cost of extending the device to operate on an extra unit per period of output.

In Figure 10.2 the analysis is put into the context of cross-media transfers of pollution. Suppose that in the uncontrolled case all emissions are to air, and that the marginal damage is represented by MD_A. It is possible to completely eradicate air pollution by the use of a wet control device, which, however, results in water pollution, the value of the damage to society being represented by MD_W. As before, the marginal cost of applying this system to successive units of output is shown by MCC.

Two new curves are now introduced. Firstly the MD_W and MCC curves are summed vertically to give the curve labelled $(MCC + MD_W)$ which represents the total marginal cost to society of the pollution caused by different output levels, when the wet control device is in operation. Clearly the cost to society has two constituents:- the cost of control and the damage remaining after control. The curve marked MPB shows simply the marginal private benefit (excluding pollution control costs) of producing the good which is the marginal revenue less the marginal cost (other than treatment cost).

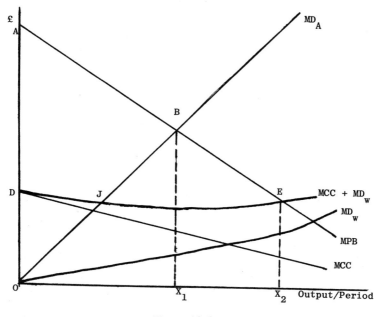

Figure 10.2

Referring again to Figure 10.2, it can be seen that there are two alternative courses of action open to society:- to use the control device, or to sacrifice some output. If the device is not utilised, then the optimal level of output is x_1 where marginal damage equals marginal private benefit. Conversely, if the device is employed, the optimal output is x_2, the level at which the marginal cost of control plus the marginal damage after control equals the marginal private benefit. The first question requiring resolution is which of these points is preferable to society.

In the case of no controls the total private benefit from output will be $OABX_1$ and the total pollution damage OBX_1, leaving a total net benefit of OAB. Where controls are used the total benefit is $OAEX_2$ from which must be deducted $ODEX_2$ leaving a net benefit of DAE. Both of these net benefit areas have a common component of DABJ:-

OAB = DABJ + ODJ   (no controls)
DAE = DABJ + JBE   (controls)

As this diagram has been drawn, JBE $>$ ODJ, so the use of the wet control device results in a larger net benefit to society than the use of no controls.

The central objective of this paper is to determine which type of public regulation of pollution externalities is most likely to result in producers' output and pollution control policies coinciding with the optimal

configuration for society. The alternative implications of imposing
environmental standards for both media, charges for both media, and
finally a standard for air and a charge for water, are considered in
this light. In all respects except the labelling of intersection points,
Figures 10.3, 10.4 and 10.5 are identical to Figure 10.2, and are reproduced
only for reasons of clarity.

If the producer decides not to employ the control device, then suppose that
his airborne emissions are controlled by a standard imposed by the competent
authority, which in the U.K. would be the H.M. Alkali Inspectorate or Local
Authority. Being responsible only for airborne emissions, one would expect
them to set the standard for mass emissions at the level where they
considered the marginal damage to be S_A in Figure 10.3. The producer's
output would therefore be constrained to OX_1, and his total profit would be
$OABX_1$.

The producer's alternative is to employ the wet control device and be
constrained in output by a standard for waterborne emissions determined
(in the U.K.) by the appropriate Regional Water Authority. Now ideally
this standard will be set at that level of marginal damage which constrains
producers to the optimal level of output. In this case, then, the
appropriate standard in terms of mass emissions to water would be the
quantity at which the marginal damage is S_w in Figure 10.3. Output is thus
constrained to OX_2, and the total net profit to the firm is $OAEX_2$ less
$ODFX_2$ which equals DAEF.

In this satanic world, producers' policies are likely to be influenced by
the magnitude of their profits rather than the well-being of society, so
that we must compare the profit figures for the two alternative strategies.
These can be divided into components below:-

$$OABX_1 = DABG + ODGX_1 \qquad \text{(no controls)}$$
$$DAEF = DABG + GBEF \qquad \text{(controls)}$$

As this diagram stands, $ODGX_1 > GBEF$, so that the profit-maximising producer
will opt for the lower output and no use of pollution controls.

Already, we have the interesting result that the imposition of standards
which seem appropriate to the regulatory agencies, will not necessarily
secure an optimal solution for society in instances where there are
potential cross-media transfers of pollution. This is not to say that
appropriate standards for this purpose do not exist — indeed it is not
difficult to perceive that the appropriate standard for air would be X_2E —
but rather that the limited role jurisdiction of separate regulatory
authorities is likely to result in inappropriate measures being taken, which
may in turn lead to a frustration of society's best interests.

Suppose now, that charges for emission of residuals are made instead of
standards being imposed. Following Coase, and Baumol and Oates, the
appropriate charge is a levy per unit of product equivalent to the marginal
damage pertaining to the final unit of output. Thus for no control, the
charge for airborne residuals will be S_A per unit, and net total profit

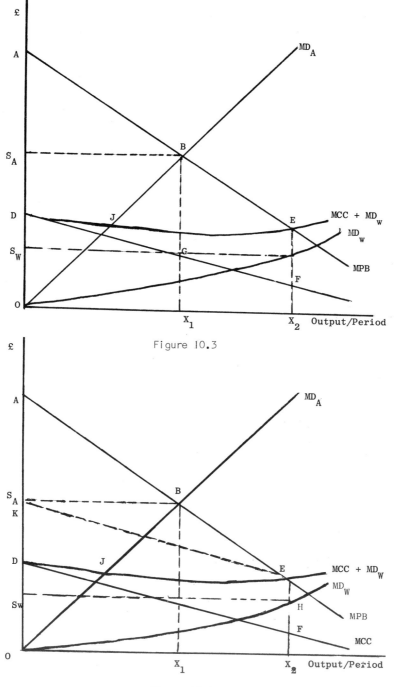

Figure 10.3

Figure 10.4

will be restricted to $S_A AB$. In the case of using the wet control device
the charge will be S_W per unit, so profit will be restricted to DAEF less
$OS_W HX_2$ in Figure 10.4. Since:-

$$DKEF = OS_W HX_2 \text{ (KE parallel) to DF, and } HX_2 = EF)$$

then profit must be KAE which is DAEF less DKEF.

But it can be seen from the diagram that:-

$$KAE > S_A AB$$

so the producer will use the wet control system, since it yields a larger
net profit.

In fact it can be demonstrated that appropriately set charges will always
result in profit maximisers making the socially optimal strategic choice.
It has been demonstrated above that in one particular case, standards did
not result in the optimal solution, whereas charges did have this effect.
The more general conclusion is that charges will always have the desired
effect, but standards may or may not have this effect. The demonstration
of the possibility of a divergence in result between standards and charges
in the case of cross-media transfers of pollution being present, is the
substantial objective of this chapter. However, before returning to discuss
the public policy implications of this result, a third possible
configuration of regulatory controls is considered.

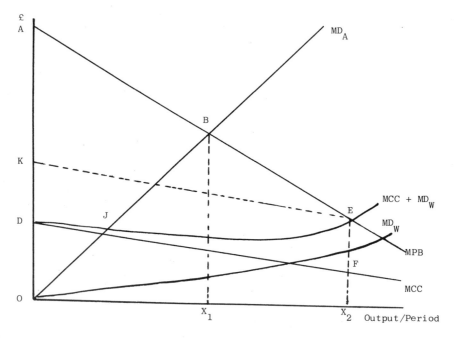

Figure 10.5

This third possibility is explored in Figure 10.5.chiefly because it seems
to reflect the reality of environmental administration in some cases. It
is where airborne emissions are controlled by a standard and waterborne
emissions by a charge, and is relevant where any waterborne effluent would
go to sewer, or as has been proposed in a number of Western countries, where
charges are made for discharges to river. In this instance, the alternative
alternatives facing the producer are profits as below:-

$$OABX_1 \qquad\qquad\qquad (\text{no controls})$$
$$DAEF - DKEF = KAE \qquad (\text{controls})$$

As can be seen from Figure 10.5,$OABX_1$ is substantially larger than KAE, so
the producer will opt for the socially inferior alternative of using no
controls. It will be apparent to the reader that such a perverse result
is much more likely in this case than in the case of standards being
applied to both air and water, since the effect of a standard is to
subsidise the creation of infra-marginal units of damage. Therefore, the
relatively high marginal damage of airborne emissions is subsidised, whilst
the lower marginal damage of waterborne effluent is charged, inevitably
resulting in a bias towards using no controls. Whilst this conclusion is in
itself quite unremarkable, its implications for public policy would seem
clear and unambiguous.

POLICY IMPLICATIONS

Whilst it is not especially surprising that the use of a standard for
controlling one medium and a charge for another can lead to a socially
sub-optimal choice of control strategies, it is more interesting to note
that such a result can also occur where standards are used for both media,
if these standards are not mutually determined. The first question to
answer is why this problem arises, and the second is why the use of
independently determined charges for each medium does not generate the
same problem.

The core of the matter is exposed by closer examination of the MCC curves
in Figures 10.2 - 10.5. If the producer decided to adopt the control device
in order to raise his output from X_1 to X_2, he pays not only for the cost
of control of X_1X_2 units, but also for the cost of the first X_1 units
which could have been produced without using pollution controls. This cost
is $ODGX_1$ in Figure 10.3 and may outweigh the extra profit from producing
the additional X_1X_2 units of output, measured by GBEF in Figure 10.3.
Conversely where charges are levied on both media, the benefit in terms of
a lower charge per unit of output will tip the balance back in favour of
using controls, where these are the optimal social strategy.

Of course, if for some doctrinaire or administrative reason charges are
deemed unacceptable, there are a number of ways of avoiding these
potential distortions. One would certainly be to find some way of
subsidising pollution control, perhaps through capital grants of some
sort, whilst another would be to direct firms to install a particular form
of equipment. However, a solution which seems preferable is to set
standards for different media simultaneously, rather than in isolation. The
appropriate standard for air in Figure 10.3 is clearly X_2E, the marginal

total cost to society of pollution if the optimal policy of using the wet
control is adopted. This is the only standard which avoids a potential
profit to producers by transferring pollution from a medium where its
marginal cost to society is lower to one where it is higher. This
uniformity can only be achieved if the agency setting the standard for
each medium has knowledge of the damage parameters of all media to which
pollution might potentially be transferred. Perhaps only some form of
national scale pollution control agency would be competent to make such
decisions.

We have, here, only indicated the possibilities for improvements in
regulatory functions in the simple case of a two medium world, where there
is only one available pollution control device. The analysis, however,
can be generalised to all three environmental media, and to any finite
number of alternative control devices. We have not developed the conditions
under which the described distortions arise, but have shown that there is a
potential for socially sub-optimal decisions to be made where standards
are used for regulation. The difficulty can be overcome either by using
charges, or by ensuring that the standards are set by an authority whose
competence extends over the whole range of environmental media.

CHAPTER 11

Conclusion

In the first chapter we noted that it was especially important to
understand and 'manage' cross-media transfers where there were positive
environmental opportunity costs of diverting wastes streams. However, it
was also suggested that cross-media transfers of pollution per se should
not really warrant any change in public policy, if, under the existing
control agencies, the standards or charges set for damage to environmental
media correctly reflect economic damage caused by pollutants. Under that
regime, firms would make their own choices about effluent disposal and
emissions. However, under a less than perfect system of either
administrative vigilance or voluntary market solutions, cross-media
transfers are likely to be a major environmental policy issue.

The guidelines we can derive from a simple micro-economic analysis of
cross-media transfers of pollution are simple enough. From the point of
view of maximising economic welfare it was shown that the basic public
policy guideline to follow was for marginal social cost (not marginal damage)
to each medium to be equalised. A unified control inspectorate with perfect
information could soon set about minimising the perverse effects of cross-
media transfers. However, not only are the administrative problems of
forming a new bureaucratic body substantial, but an integrated control
authority may be unlikely to be party to perfect information on the economic
impact of environmental damage. We have already noted those situations
whereby control of airborne emissions in, for instance, iron and steel and
primary aluminium may reduce emissions of one set of pollutants like iron
oxide and fluoride but through the use of extra energy, to drive the
necessary building evacuation control plants, they may actually be a net
creator of other airborne pollutants.

We have in this book postulated an alternative approach to the usual one
of measuring environmental damage. Whilst this is subject to considerable
conceptual problems it seems certain that unless some way of measuring
economic damage from pollution is made, then a public policy stance
towards cross-media transfers will be unlikely to be much of an improvement
on the system we already have. The only alternative approach is to set
ambient standards for various environmental media on the basis of
technological, political and economic judgements (as they are now) and
then direct effluent streams in such a way as to achieve these environmental

113

standards at minimum cost. This merely requires knowledge of abatement costs
and efficiencies and does not involve complicated economic damage evaluation.
This is of course the implication that stems from the work of Kneese and
Bower mentioned in Chapter I.

In view of the importance of their work it is worth, at this stage, making
a review of their approach and basic results, although the reader is
strongly advised to read a recent book which reviews in detail the
research. (I) Not surprisingly their analysis, too, has as its starting
point the Law of Conservation of Mass:

> "Conservation of mass dictates that the weight of a
> residuals stream once generated cannot be reduced by
> modification. In fact, mass is increased, as well as is
> the quantity of energy residuals, because the modification
> process itself requires inputs. Modification processes
> can only: (a) change a residual into another type of the
> same form; (b) change the form, for example, from
> liquid to solid; (c) change the time, or location (or
> both) of discharge; and (d) any combination of (a), (b),
> and (c). Further, production process changes that
> reduce discharges to one medium, even though they can
> reduce the total mass of residuals generated, may increase
> residuals flow to another medium. Accordingly, liquid,
> solid, gaseous, and energy residuals streams are
> generally interdependent, and the cost of modifying one
> will depend to a greater or lesser degree on the
> constraints imposed upon discharges of the others."

They go on to suggest that recycling can reduce materials flow but not
stop it and that ultimately the driving force behind their 'Residuals
Environmental Quality Management model' (REQM) is the final demand for
goods and services in society - including the spatial distribution of
activities, product mix and the 'life style' of society. Our conclusions,
although not based on any regional evaluation, would basically support this.
The importance of their work, however, is that it was attempted within a
closed system (The Lower Delaware Valley) and thus interlinkages in the
system were constrained and this made evaluation more easy to handle.

The general conclusions emmanating from this work are much in line with
our own. In particular that REQM is affected by a wide range of decisions
made by individual economic units making choices on types of material,
energy inputs, process technology, extent of materials recovery and the
overall level and time pattern of the production of goods, services
and energy. Since all these are subject to price changes the optimal
level of activity and discharge may change rapidly over time. Thus REQM
takes place in a dynamic context that has continually changing factor
price, technology, product mix, product specification and social tastes.
Because of this dynamic background the mathematical models developed by
the Resources for the Future researchers modeled quantitatively various
factors such as the likely responses to charges and restrictions on the
discharge of residuals to the environment; likely responses to changes in
the prices, both absolute and relative, of various factor inputs; and how
these responses differ between existing and new activities.

However overall REQM costs in a region are affected by REQM objectives.
Since these were framed in terms of ambient environmental quality

standards, the analysis at once becomes feasible but arguably less valuable since the objectives are themselves the result of administrative and political decisions rather than some dynamic cost-benefit maximisation. It must be noted however that our own approach in Chapters 7 and 8 suffer similar drawbacks although in a different context. In addition it might be claimed that it is less general and embracing.

There is little doubt that with the right methodology and models for evaluation, cross media transfers because they are pervasive, should be a central theme in the administration of environmental controls. To ignore them will lead to underinvestment in pollution control. However to change the basis on which control agencies work might not lead to very major gains. In the case studies we reviewed it seems that in the Fertilizer industry there were potential problems but there was little major evidence of the inadequacies and distortions of the existing system. Our review of discharges of scrubbing water to river and sewers led us to similar conclusions. In the case of steel, iron, and primary aluminium the case was less clear and it seemed likely that some change in administrative stance could improve environmental quality and change the nature and extent of cross media transfers.

However the mere provision of an integrated management system is itself no guarantee of change or improvement and indeed might reduce vigilance over perverse pollution transfers once they had been accepted into the environmental system. It seems likely that most countries will move slowly towards some integrated system but the speed with which they move should take note of the feasibility of running a large bureaucratic integrated management system (to take account of resourse development as well?) and the likely costs and benefits of change. All residuals are at some time subject to cross media movement, the important point is to focus attention on those which are being diverted to waste stream which, in the long run, create more damage through the secondary and indirect cross-media effects.

REFERENCES

1. Kneese, A.V. and Bower, B.T. (1979) Environmental Quality and
      Residuals Management. Resources for the Future. John Hopkins,
      University Press.

APPENDIX

Project Information

OBJECTIVE

The use of pollution control devices in industry to reduce a stream of residuals, often results in the creation of a secondary residual stream. Pollution may be transferred from one medium to another (for example from air to water, or water to solid), so that the environmental effect of particular control measures may not be confined to their direct impact on emissions of the primary pollutant. It is for this reason that we are attempting to develop a methodology for analysing the overall environmental impact of alternative pollution control measures. We are of the opinion that the use of objective 'cost-benefit' type methods of assessing damage caused by different pollutants is, because of technological complexities, often inappropriate for this kind of comparison. In such cases it may be better to adopt a subjective approach, enlisting the assistance of individuals who are expert in different aspects of the effects of pollution.

METHODOLOGY

In order to compare alternative pollution control measures for a particular production process, involving different configurations of emissions to air, water and land, it is necessary for some form of 'weights' to be attached to the effect of each pollutant. Of course the damage caused by a particular pollutant will depend on a large number of factors - quantity, concentration, location, etc. - and it is not possible for us to specify every relevant variable. Indeed it is the very intractability of the problem in technological terms that has led us to believe that the subjective opinions of experts are the soundest bases for analysis. Nevertheless we do make assumptions about quantity, concentration, and location, which are described in Item 2.

Each participant is asked to rank and weight the list of pollutants (Item 3) on the basis of the assumptions specified in Item 2. Although some of the pollutants are airborne, some waterborne and some solid, they should be treated as one list, since an important aim of the exercise is to assess the relative damage done by emissions to different media. Experts are also

asked questions (Item 4) about the airborne and waterborne pollutants,
which are intended to give an idea of the damage functions for each of
these substances. The list of pollutants has been compiled to include the
most important general emissions from industrial processes in the UK as
well as some which are important in particular industries which we intend
to study in more detail. Finally, participants are given the (entirely
optional) opportunity to make any brief comments they wish in explanation
of their weightings.

After the replies of all participants have been analysed, each expert will
be sent a document showing the median weightings of all individuals
alongside his own weightings, and perhaps also some of the comments made
by other participants which will be reproduced anonymously and in stylised
form. Each expert will then be invited to confirm or amend his previously
expressed view in the light of this information. This process may or may
not then be repeated one further time, depending upon the degree of
consensus existing.

SOME COMMENTS

It is our opinion that the 'Delphi' type technique using subjective
criteria is appropriate to a study of the environmental effects of
different pollutants, though so far as we are aware, this is the first
time such an exercise has been attempted in the UK. The problem of
pollution is so far-reaching in its scope that no one person, however
eminent in his own field, could be expert in every aspect of the subject.
We feel that the 'Delphi' technique, in addition to its other advantages,
allows individuals to confirm views they hold strongly, and amend those
held only tentatively.

No doubt many people will consider that we are asking for 'easy' answers
to difficult questions, and in a sense many of the questions have no
single answer. Nevertheless our objective is the testing of a methodology,
and since both public and private bodies are continually making implicit
relative valuations of different forms of pollution, there seems to be
merit in making some explicit weightings, even though these will
undoubtedly fall short of any great degree of precision. We hope that,
after the completion of this section of our work, both the methodology
and the results will be the subject of constructive criticism, so that
future work might be directed at making some appropriate refinements.

ITEM 2

INSTRUCTIONS FOR MAKING WEIGHTINGS

Please make the following assumptions:-

A. The location is an urban area of the UK. Present in the locality are
    these industries

    (i).   Fertiliser manufacture
    (ii)   Power generation
    (iii) Iron founding
    (iv)   Iron and steel manufacture
    (v)   Metal finishing
    (vi)   A selection of other heavy industry

B. All liquid effluents are discharged to one river, which is non-tidal,
    has a flow rate of 6,000 million litres/day (1,300 million gals/day),
    and reaches the open sea 30 miles below our specified location. Its
    chemical condition is Class 2 - "Doubtful" quality - under the D.O.E.
    classification.

C. All airborne discharges are made at the concentration shown below, and
    through a stack which is 100ft. high.

Pollutants	Concentration
Ammonia	5 p.p.m.
Fluorides	20 mg/m^3 (0.009 gr/ft^3)
Heavy metals	100 mg/m^3 (0.044 gr/ft^3)
Hydrogen sulphide	5 p.p.m.
Nitrogen oxides	1,000 p.p.m.
Total organics	100 p.p.m.
Particulates	0.5 gm/m^3 (0.2.8 gr/ft^3)
Sulphur dioxide	4 gm/m^3 (1.747 gr/ft^3)

D. Solid wastes are deposited on licensed sites, or disposed of in the
    way most appropriate. Fertiliser sludge can be assumed to emanate
    from granulation scrubbers, and iron founding sludge from a gas c
    cleaning plant. Metal finishing sludge may be assumed to consist
    largely of metal hydroxides. All sludges may be considered suspensions
    of solids in excess of 2%.

E. The basis for comparison of the pollutants is the emission of 100 lb/hr
    of each (with the exception of heat).

Now please refer to Item 3 (List of Pollutants)

This set of pollutants, including airborne, waterborne and solid, should be read as one list. You will notice that the same chemical substance discharged to a different medium is treated as a different pollutant. Please follow these steps:-

(1) Rank the 26 pollutants in order of descending importance 1-26. This ranking should take account of the overall environmental effect of discharges of the specified amount of each pollutant, given the assumptions above. Insert your rankings in Column 4, marking the most damaging pollutant 1, and the least damaging 26.

(2) In Column 5 write 100% against the pollutant ranked 1. Then try to assess the importance of each of the other pollutants as a percentage of the most important. Insert this estimate (between 0% and 100%) in Column 5 for those pollutants ranked 2-26. Clearly those pollutants ranked higher in (1) will have higher percentages attached to them than those ranked lowly. If you consider that any substance listed is not a pollutant at all, write 0 in Column 5.

(3) If there are any brief comments you would like to make concerning your weightings or rankings, please write these in the space provided on the reverse side of Item 3.

Now please refer to Item 4

This is a series of questions, for each airborne and waterborne pollutant, designed to give an indication of the form of the damage function of the particular substance. You are asked to fill in the 4 gaps for each pollutant. If, for example, you believe that the damage caused by a particular substance is exactly proportional to the quantity emitted, then you would insert in the gaps as follows:

(i)   An emission of 10 lb/hr would be 0.1 times as damaging as 100 lb/hr
(ii)   An emission of 50 lb/hr would be 0.5 times as damaging as 100 lb/hr
(iii) An emission of 1,000 lb/hr would be 10 times as damaging as 100 lb/hr
(iv)   An emission of 1,000 lb/hr would be 100 times as damaging as 100 lb/hr.

If you believe a particular level of emission to be negligible or infinitely large in importance, then please insert "0" or "infinitely" as appropriate. These values should be based on the same assumptions as were made for the relative weightings in Item 3.

When you have completed these steps, please return Items 3 and 4 to us in the envelope provided.

Appendix

ITEM 3

LIST OF POLLUTANTS

1 POLLUTANT	2 MEDIUM	3 EMISSION QLTY	4 RANKING	5 % of HIGHEST
Ammonia	Air	100 lb/hr		
Fluorides	Air	100 lb/hr		
Heavy metals	Air	100 lb/hr		
Hydrogen sulphide	Air	100 lb/hr		
Nitrogen oxides	Air	100 lb/hr		
Total organics	Air	100 lb/hr		
Particulates	Air	100 lb/hr		
Sulphur dioxide	Air	100 lb/hr		
Ammonia	Water	100 lb/hr		
Fluorides	Water	100 lb/hr		
Heavy metals	Water	100 lb/hr		
Suspended solids (other than heavy metals + arsenic compounds)	Water	100 lb/hr		
Oil and grease	Water	100 lb/hr		
Nitrates	Water	100 lb/hr		
Phenols	Water	100 lb/hr		
Phosphates	Water	100 lb/hr		
Cyanides	Water	100 lb/hr		
Sulphates	Water	100 lb/hr		
Sulphides	Water	100 lb/hr		
Heat	Water	100,000,000 (10^8)BTU/hr		
Fertiliser sludge	Solid	100 lb/hr		
Iron founding sludge	Solid	100 lb/hr		
Coal ash	Solid	100 lb/hr		
Gypsum	Solid	100 lb/hr		
Slag	Solid	100 lb/hr		

SPACE FOR COMMENTS CONCERNING WEIGHTINGS

ITEM 4

AMMONIA (Air)

  (i)   An emission of 10 lb/hr would be   .. times as damaging as 100 lb/hr
  (ii)   An emission of 50 lb/hr would be   .. times as damaging as 100 lb/hr
  (iii) An emission of 1,000 lb/hr would be   .. times as damaging as 100 lb/hr
  (iv)   An emission of 10,000 lb/hr would be   .. times as damaging as 100 lb/hr

FLUORIDES (Air)

  (i)   An emission of 10 lb/hr would be   .. times as damaging as 100 lb/hr
  (ii)   An emission of 50 lb/hr would be   .. times as damaging as 100 lb/hr
  (iii) An emission of 1,000 lb/hr would be   .. times as damaging as 100 lb/hr
  (iv)   An emission of 10,000 lb/hr would be   .. times as damaging as 100 lb/hr

HEAVY METALS (Air)

  (i)   An emission of 10 lb/hr would be   .. times as damaging as 100 lb/hr
  (ii)   An emission of 50 lb/hr would be   .. times as damaging as 100 lb/hr
  (iii) An emission of 1,000 lb/hr would be   .. times as damaging as 100 lb/hr
  (iv)   An emission of 10,000 lb/hr would be   .. times as damaging as 100 lb/hr

HYDROGEN SULPHIDE (Air)

  (i)   An emission of 10 lb/hr would be   .. times as damaging as 100 lb/hr
  (ii)   An emission of 50 lb/hr would be   .. times as damaging as 100 lb/hr
  (iii) An emission of 1,000 lb/hr would be   .. times as damaging as 100 lb/hr
  (iv)   An emission of 10,000 lb/hr would be   .. times as damaging as 100 lb/hr

NITROGEN OXIDES (Air)

  (i)   An emission of 10 lb/hr would be   .. times as damaging as 100 lb/hr
  (ii)   An emission of 50 lb/hr would be   .. times as damaging as 100 lb/hr
  (iii) An emission of 1,000 lb/hr would be   .. times as damaging as 100 lb/hr
  (iv)   An emission of 10,000 lb/hr would be   .. times as damaging as 100 lb/hr

PARTICULATES (Air)

  (i)   An emission of 10 lb/hr would be   .. times as damaging as 100 lb/hr
  (ii)   An emission of 50 lb/hr would be   .. times as damaging as 100 lb/hr
  (iii) An emission of 1,000 lb/hr would be   .. times as damaging as 100 lb/hr
  (iv)   An emission of 10,000 lb/hr would be   .. times as damaging as 100 lb/hr

SULPHUR DIOXIDE (Air)

  (i)   An emission of 10 lb/hr would be   .. times as damaging as 100 lb/hr
  (ii)   An emission of 50 lb/hr would be   .. times as damaging as 100 lb/hr
  (iii) An emission of 1,000 lb/hr would be   .. times as damaging as 100 lb/hr
  (iv)   An emission of 10,000 lb/hr would be   .. times as damaging as 100 lb/hr

TOTAL ORGANICS (Air)

(i)   An emission of 10 lb/hr would be   .. times as damaging as 100 lb/hr
(ii)   An emission of 50 lb/hr would be   .. times as damaging as 100 lb/hr
(iii) An emission of 1,000 lb/hr would be   .. times as damaging as 100 lb/hr
(iv)   An emission of 10,000 lb/hr would be .. times as damaging as 100 lb/hr

FLUORIDES (Water)

(i)   An emission of 10 lb/hr would be   .. times as damaging as 100 lb/hr
(ii)   An emission of 50 lb/hr would be   ...times as damaging as 100 lb/hr
(iii) An emission of 1,000 lb/hr would be   .. times as damaging as 100 lb/hr
(iv)   An emission of 10,000 lb/hr would be .. times as damaging as 100 lb/hr

HEAVY METALS (Water)

(i)   An emission of 10 lb/hr would be   .. times as damaging as 100 lb/hr
(ii)   An emission of 50 lb/hr would be   .. times as damaging as 100 lb/hr
(iii) An emission of 1,000 lb/hr would be   .. times as damaging as 100 lb/hr
(iv)   An emission of 10,000 lb/hr would be .. times as damaging as 100 lb/hr

SUSPENDED SOLIDS (other than heavy metals or Arsenic) Water)

(i)   An emission of 10,lb/hr would be   .. times as damaging as 100 lb/hr
(ii)   An emission of 50 lb/hr would be   .. times as damaging as 100 lb/hr
(iii) An emission of 1,000 lb/hr would be   .. times as damaging as 100 lb/hr
(iv)   An emission of 10,000 lb/hr would be .. times as damaging as 100 lb/hr

OIL AND GREASE (Water)

(i)   An emission of 10 lb/hr would be   .. times as damaging as 100 lb/hr
(ii)   An emission of 50 lb/hr would be   .. times as damaging as 100 lb/hr
(iii) An emission of 1,000 lb/hr would be   .. times as damaging as 100 lb/hr
(iv)   An emission of 10,000 lb/hr would be .. times as damaging as 100 lb/hr

NITRATES (Water)

(i)   An emission of 10 lb/hr would be   .. times as damaging as 100 lb/hr
(ii)   An emission of 50 lb/hr would be   .. times as damaging as 100 lb/hr
(iii) An emission of 1,000 lb/hr would be   .. times as damaging as 100 lb/hr
(iv)   An emission of 10,000 lb/hr would be .. times as damaging as 100 lb/hr

PHENOLS (Water)

(i)   An emission of 10 lb/hr would be   .. times as damaging as 100 lb/hr
(ii)   An emission of 50 lb/hr would be   .. times as damaging as 100 lb/hr
(iii) An emission of 1,000 lb/hr would be   .. times as damaging as 100 lb/hr
(iv)   An emission of 10,000 lb/hr would be .. times as damaging as 100 lb/hr

PHOSPHATES (Water)

  (i)   An emission of 10 lb/hr would be   .. times as damaging as 100 lb/hr
  (ii)   An emission of 50 lb/hr would be   .. times as damaging as 100 lb/hr
 (iii) An emission of 1,000 lb/hr would be .. times as damaging as 100 lb/hr
  (iv) An emission of 10,000 lb/hr would be .. times as damaging as 100 lb/hr

CYANIDES (Water)

  (i)   An emission of 10 lb/hr would be   .. times as damaging as 100 lb/hr
  (ii)   An emission of 50 lb/hr would be   .. times as damaging as 100 lb/hr
 (iii) An emission of 1,000 lb/hr would be .. times as damaging as 100 lb/hr
  (iv) An emission of 10,000 lb/hr would be .. times as damaging as 100 lb/hr

SULPHATES (Water)

  (i)   An emission of 10 lb/hr would be   .. times as damaging as 100 lb/hr
  (ii)   An emission of 50 lb/hr would be   .. times as damaging as 100 lb/hr
 (iii) An emission of 1,000 lb/hr would be .. times as damaging as 100 lb/hr
  (iv) An emission of 10,000 lb/hr would be .. times as damaging as 100 lb/hr

SULPHIDES (Water)

  (i)   An emission of 10 lb/hr would be   .. times as damaging as 100 lb/hr
  (ii)   An emission of 50 lb/hr would be   .. times as damaging as 100 lb/hr
 (iii) An emission of 1,000 lb/hr would be .. times as damaging as 100 lb/hr
  (iv) An emission of 10,000 lb/hr would be .. times as damaging as 100 lb/hr

AMMONIA (Water)

  (i)   An emission of 10 lb/hr would be   .. times as damaging as 100 lb/hr
  (ii)   An emission of 50 lb/hr would be   .. times as damaging as 100 lb/hr
 (iii) An emission of 1,000 lb/hr would be .. times as damaging as 100 lb/hr
  (iv) An emission of 10,000 lb/hr would be .. times as damaging as 100 lb/hr.

Author Index

Ayres, R.U.   3,99,113

Barber, J.E.   61
Baumol, W.J.   108
Bower, B.T.   8,113-116

Coase, R   108
Cooper, H   61

Green, W   61

Honea, F.I.   53

Kelley, R   8
Kneese, A.V.   3,8,99,113

Lewis, D.C.   68
Lowe, J.F.   68

Oates, W   108

Pearce, D.W.   66

Russell, C.S.   8

Spofford, W.O.   8
Stairmand, C.J.   55

Subject Index